Beautiful Embroidered & Embellished Knits

by
Jane Davis

Library of Congress
Catalog Number:
ISBN: 0-9678033-0-6

Printed in the
United States of America

Technical editing

Lois Varga of
Anacapa Fine Yarns
4572 Telephone Road #909
Ventura, CA 93003
(805) 654-9500
www.anacapafineyarns.com

Corinne Loomer, teacher at
Creative Castle
2321 Michael Drive
Newbury Park, CA 92320
(805) 499-1377
www.creativecastle.com

Questions or comments about this book?
Email Jane Davis at beads@anacapa.net
Be sure to put "Book Question" in the subject line.

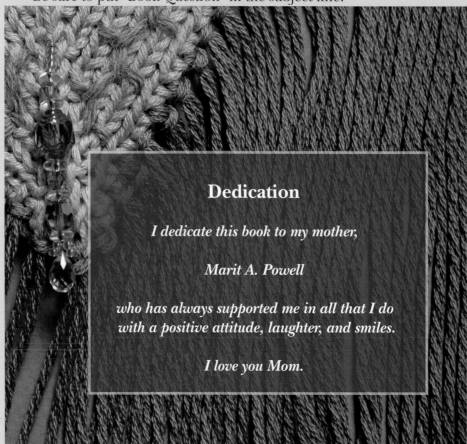

Dedication

I dedicate this book to my mother,

Marit A. Powell

who has always supported me in all that I do with a positive attitude, laughter, and smiles.

I love you Mom.

Many Thanks

Putting a book together takes a great deal of time and energy. I enjoy most parts of the process, but I couldn't have done it without the help and encouragement of those around me. I am very grateful to a number of people who have helped me to get this book to print.

First and foremost, I would like to thank my mother, Marit A. Powell, for her positive, easy going attitude, and for teaching me to have fun and to enjoy life.

I will always be beholden to Carole Tripp, owner of Creative Castle bead store in Newbury Park, California. She has always been a supportive force for me, with a positive attitude and an honest, friendly demeanor that I truly treasure in business or personal circumstances. And thanks for coming up with the title of this book!

Lois Varga, owner of Anacapa Fine Yarns in Ventura, California, is a wonderful person, who has been a joy to work with and get to know as she painstakingly edited this book in the height of the holiday season, and beyond, answering questions on details and providing excellent suggestions to make this book better with each edit.

Corinne Loomer is a talented beadwork teacher, knitter and friend, who agreed at the last minute to look over these pages for added accuracy. Thanks for your help and support!

The editors and art departments at Lark Books and Krause Publishing have taught me many details over the years to help me create a quality book.

The following yarn companies' fabulous yarns inspired the projects in this book

Berroco, Inc
Brown Sheep Co., Inc.
Blue Sky Alpacas, Inc.
Cascade Yarns
Classic Elite Yarns
Dale of Norway
Harrisville Designs
Jaeger
Koigu
Lorna's Laces Yarns
Louisa Harding
Mountain Colors
Patons
Plymouth
Rowan
S. Charles Collezione
Tahki/Stacy Charles
Trendsetter Yarns

And finally thank you to my family, Richard, Jeff, Andrew, and Jonathan,
who have all lived with me and my yarn, and beads, and fabric
through small piles and tall piles (mostly tall piles!).
I love you dearly.

Table of Contents

Introduction

How can you create a knitting project with fabulous, detailed designs, rich in color, pattern and texture, but without complex color sequences or detailed texture patterns that demand close concentration while knitting? Easy. You simply knit the project first in easy Stockinette stitch, then embellish it with embroidery when your knitting is through! It's a great way to add color and texture to your finished knitwear. From simply sewing on a few beads, to intricate detailed embroidery designs, you can choose to make quick and easy projects, or heirlooms to cherish. Since the embroidery is the focal point of the project, you can spend your knitting time on easy stockinette projects, enjoying the beautiful yarn and concentrating on time with friends and family, rather than difficult stitches. When your project is completed, then you add the finishing details to make it shine.

Here are thirty projects, primarily knit in Stockinette stitch, which you then embellish with a variety of techniques including embroidery, bead embellishment, Swiss darning (also known as duplicate stitch), and appliqué. You'll find several projects in each technique, ranging from quick and easy embellishments to challenging designs. Also, there are projects that combine one or more different techniques such as Swiss darning and bead edgings.

But don't stop here. The beauty of this technique is that it's transferable to other projects! Take a favorite knitwear pattern and add an appliqué flower or easy Swiss darned zigzag. Or, if you're in a pinch for something to wear, but don't want the generic store bought sweater, you can make it your own with a quick embellishment of beads or a sprinkling of flowers. Whichever you choose, I hope that this book helps you to enjoy the yarn and enjoy your time knitting and embellishing!

Section 1
Basics

Following is a quick review reference of knitting terms and techniques, as well as an overall description of the embroidery techniques and tools for the projects in this book.

Abbreviations

Abbreviations save room and can help make reading patterns simpler, once you are familiar with their meanings. The following abbreviations were used mostly for the intermediate to advanced patterns in this book. Where there was room, and especially in the easier patterns, I have tried to avoid using a lot of abbreviations so that the patterns are easier to follow.

Approx	Approximately
beg	begin, begins, beginning
BO	bind off
cir	circular
cm	centimeter (2.5 = 1 inch)
CO	cast on
cont	continue
dec	decrease, decreases, decreasing
dpn	double pointed needle, double pointed needles
foll	following
ea	each
g	gram, grams
Gt st	Garter Stitch
inc	increase, increases, increasing
k	knit
k2tog	knit two stitches together as one
meas	measure, measures
mm	millimeter, millimeters
oz	ounce
p	purl
patt	pattern
pm	place marker
p2tog	purl two stitches together as one
rem	remain, remains, remaining
rep	repeat, repeats
rnd(s)	round, rounds
skp	slip one, knit one, pass slipped stitch over knitted stitch
s2kp	slip two together as one, knit one, pass slipped stitches over knitted stitch
sl	slip
st(s)	stitch, stitches
St st	Stockinette Stitch
tog	together
yd(s)	yard, yards
yo	yarn over

Knitting Needle Sizes

Following is a list of knitting needle sizes in U.S. and metric (mm) sizing. There can be variances between the same size U.S. needle from company to company. That is why some of the U.S. sizes have more than one possible metric size. You may want to check the millimeter size first to make sure you have the needle you want. These aren't necessarily the only sizes available. Some oddball sized needles that might fit between some of these sizes also crop up from time to time.

U.S.	Metric
0	2 mm
1	2.25 mm
2	2.75 mm
3	3 mm or 3.25 mm
4	3.5 mm
5	3.75 mm
6	4 mm or 4.25 mm
7	4.5 mm
8	5 mm
9	5.5 mm
10	6 mm
10$_{1/2}$	6.5 mm
11	8 mm
13	9 mm
15	10 mm
17	12 mm or 12.75 mm
19	15 mm
35	19 mm or 20 mm

Knitting Stitch Patterns Used in This Book

Here are the stitches used for the majority of knitting in these patterns. Stockinette stitch is the primary stitch, though several, usually more advanced projects, have sections of Garter stitch, Ribbing, or Seed stitch. A few projects use a variation of seed stitch for added texture.

Stockinette Stitch
Knit the right side rows, purl the wrong side rows. Creates a smooth surface on the right side and a bumpy texture on the wrong side.

Garter Stitch
Knit every row. Creates a reversable fabric made of horizontal ridges on both sides of the finished knitting.

Ribbing
A reversable fabric of vertical ridges are created by working the same repeat on every right side row, such as knit 2, purl 2. Then all other rows, purl the stitches that were knitted and knit the stitches that were purled on the previous row.

Seed Stitch
A reversable bumpy textured stitch created by a repeat of knit 1, purl 1 on all right side rows. Then on each following row, knit the stitches that were knitted and purl the stitches that were purled on the previous row.

8

Symbol Guides

The handy symbols below will tell you the type of yarn used for the projects and the suggested skill level needed to complete the project. The first two charts are provided by the Yarn Council of America, while the last one I put together to help you determine if a project is one you want to tackle from the embroidery end of the skill level.

Standard Yarn Weight Guide

Here is the current industry guideline used for classifying yarn weights and average gauge and needle sizes used for each type of yarn. For every project, you will find a yarn symbol next to the yarns in the materials list showing the yarn weight according to this chart.

Yarn Weight Symbols	SUPER FINE 1 SUPER FIN Super Fino	FINE 2 FIN Fino	LIGHT 3 LEGER Ligero	MEDIUM 4 MOYEN Medio	BULKY 5 BULKY Abultado	SUPER BULKY 6 SUPER BULKY Super Abultado
Yarn Type	Sock, Fingering, Baby	Sport, Baby	DK, Light Worsted	Worsted, Afghan, Aran	Chunky, Craft, Rug	Bulky, Roving
Knitted Gauge in St st over 4"	27 to 32 sts	23 to 26 sts	21 to 24 sts	16 to 20 sts	12 to 15 sts	6 to 11 sts
Metric Needle Size Range	2.25mm to 3.25mm	3.25mm to 3.75mm	3.75mm to 4.5mm	4.5mm to 5.5mm	5.5mm to 8mm	8mm and larger
U. S. Needle Size Range	#1 to #3	#3 to #5	#5 to #7	#7 to #9	#9 to #11	#11 and larger

Knitting Skill Level Guide

This chart is the current industry guideline used for classifying skill levels needed to complete knitting projects. Look for the symbols at the beginning of each project which will help guide you to which projects are easy and which are more challenging.

Skill Level Symbols	Description
Beginner	Projects for first-time knitters, using basic knit and purl stitches and minimal shaping.
Easy	Projects using basic stitches, repetitive stitch patterns, simple color changes, and simple shaping and finishing.
Intermediate	Projects with a variety of stitches, such as basic cables and lace, simple intarsia, double pointed needles and knitting in the round needle techniques, plus mid-level shaping and finishing.
Experienced	Projects using advanced techniques and stitches, such as short rows, fair isle, more intricate intarsia, cables, lace patterns, plus numerous color changes.

Stitching Skill Level Guide

Each project in this book has a skill level for the knitting and a separate skill level for the embroidery/ embellishment. The knitting skill level is based on the guides provided by the Yarn Council of America. I have worked up a similar stitching guideline so you can gauge the skill level needed for the embroidery/embellishment portions of the projects.

Skill Level Symbols	Description
Beginner	Projects for first-time embroiderers, using basic stitches and basic finishing techniques.
Easy	Projects using basic stitches, repetitive stitch patterns, simple designs and easy finishing techniques.
Intermediate	Projects with a variety of stitches, more time consuming projects, plus mid-level finishing techniques.
Experienced	Projects using advanced stitching techniques, intricate detailed designs and complex finishing techniques.

Basic Knitting Techniques
- Here is a short refresher of some basic knitting techniques.

Cast On (long-tail)
Make a slip knot and place it on the needle. Hold the needle in your right hand. Wrap the tail end of yarn around your left thumb, and the working yarn around your left index finger, holding both yarns together in your other left hand fingers as shown at right. *Pass the needle under the yarn in front of your left thumb, and behind the yarn in front of your index finger. Drop the yarn off your thumb, pull both ends of yarn to tighten the new stitch on the needle. Position the yarn over your left thumb and index finger again, repeat from asterisk for each cast on stitch.

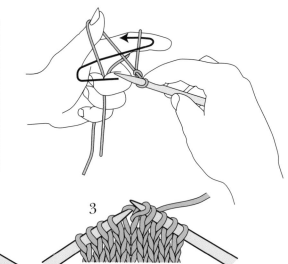

Knit Stitch
Insert the right needle into the front of the first stitch on the left needle from front to back (1). Wrap the yarn, counter-clockwise, around the right needle (2). Pull the wrapped yarn through the stitch, sliding the old stitch off the left needle as you pull the new stitch through (3).

Purl Stitch
Insert the right needle into the front of the first stitch on the left needle from back to front (1). Wrap the yarn, counter-clockwise, around the right needle (2). Pull the wrapped yarn through the stitch, sliding the old stitch off the left needle as you pull the new stitch through (3).

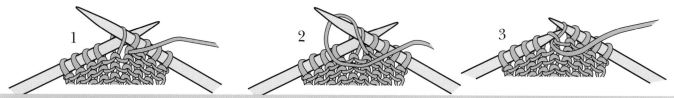

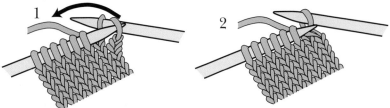

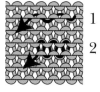

Bind Off
Work the first two stitches. Using the left needle, pick up the first stitch on the right needle (1) and pull it over the other stitch and off the needle (2). Work the next stitch. Repeat the first step of picking up the first stitch on the right needle and passing it over and off the needle. Continue until you have one stitch left on the right needle. Cut the yarn and pull through the last stitch.

Weave in Ends
Cut the tail of yarn to about 3" or 4" and thread with a tapestry needle. Pass through to the back side of the work and pass over and under the stitches (1), or follow the path of the stitches to make the tail less noticeable (2).

I-Cord
Using double pointed needles, cast on 3 to 6 stitches. Knit one row. *Keeping the knit side of the work facing you, slide the stitches to the right end of the needle. Pull the working yarn behind the knitting and knit another row. Repeat from the asterisk until the cord is the desired length. Cut the working yarn to about 6", thread with a tapestry needle and pass through the stitches from left to right.

Decreases

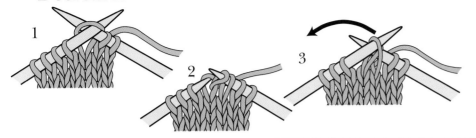

Slip-Knit-Pass Over - *A left slanting decrease.*
Slip the next stitch, as if to knit, from the left needle to the right needle (1). Knit the next stitch (2). Pass the slipped stitch over the knitted stitch, and off the needle (3).

Knit 2 Together - *A right slanting decrease.*
Insert the right needle into the front of 2 stitches on the left needle and knit them as if they were one stitch.

Increases

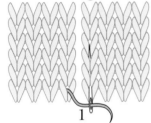

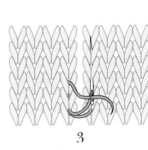

Yarn Over - *An increase that makes a hole, used for eyelets and lace.*
Wrap the yarn counter-clockwise around the right needle before working the next stitch. Work the wrapped stitch the same as a normal stitch in the pattern on the next row.

Knit in Front & Back - *An increase that forms a small horizontal ridge.*
Work a knit stitch but don't slide the old stitch off the left needle. Insert the right needle into the back of the old stitch and make a knit stitch into it, then slide the old stitch off the left needle.

Assembling Pieces

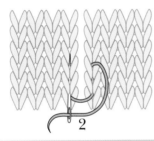

Mattress Stitch - *For joining two pieces of finished knitting, usually along the sides as shown, but also for shoulder seams.*
Lay pieces side by side with right side of fabric facing you. Thread a 24" length of yarn with a tapestry needle and attach yarn so working end is coming out of first row of knitting on left piece of knitting, half a stitch from edge. Pass under 1 or 2 rows of knitting half a stitch in from edge on right piece (1). Pass under same rows on left piece (2). *Insert needle where yarn is exiting on other piece of knitting, coming out 1 or 2 rows above (3). Repeat from asterisk several times, then gently pull yarn snuggly so knitting pulls together, hiding seam (4). Don't pull too tightly or your seam will pucker.

Grafting (Kitchener stitch) - *For joining two pieces of knitting together, sewing the live stitches together off the needles.*
Position the two pieces as shown at left. Cut the working yarn on the bottom piece to 4 times as long as the stitches to be grafted and thread it with a tapestry needle. Pass through the 1st stitch on the top piece. Pass through the 1st and 2nd stitches on the bottom piece, then the 1st and 2nd stitches on the top piece (1). Pass through the 2nd and 3rd stitches on the bottom piece (2). Continue across, always entering the 1st stitch from front to back and the 2nd stitch from back to front, and sliding the needles out of the stitches as you finish passing through them (3). Try to keep the tension of the stitches the same as that of the knitting so that the row of stitching blends in, becoming just another row of knitting.

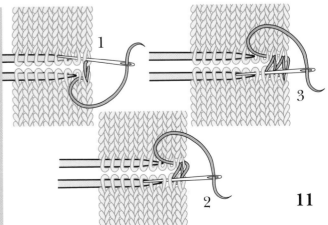

A Note About Gauge and Yarn

Gauge, or the number of stitches and rows over 4" of knitting, is very important in anything you need to match exactly to the instructions, such as sweaters and hats that need to end up a specific size. For these items it is imperative that you make a test swatch in the yarn and needles you plan to use and measure to make sure the gauge is the same as listed for the project. If there are too many stitches, then you will need to make another swatch using larger needles. If there are too few stitches, then you will need to try again with smaller needles. If you just can't get the right gauge, you will need to follow the pattern diagram, beginning with enough stitches to get the correct width of the piece, and measuring as you go to get the correct length. But this process of working through a pattern from the chart alone is not for beginners, so it's always best to begin with the proper gauge. You will also find that using metal, plastic and wood needles will all have different effects on the knitted gauge. From my experience, yarn on wood doesn't slide as easily and the gauge is a little more loose than with metal needles. So if your gauge is close, you might try the same size needle in a different material to see if that changes your gauge. I do recommend using the same yarn as was used in the projects because it is more likely that you will have the same results, although substitutions can work if you take time to get the correct gauge. Scarves and pillows are not quite as crucial, since it won't matter too much if your scarf is a little longer or wider than the instructions. A pillow might need a different sized pillow form, but it will still be a nice pillow, even if it wasn't made to gauge.

Blocking

Blocking sets the size of the knitting, evens out the stitches somewhat, and can minimize the curling that naturally occurs on the sides and ends of Stockinette stitch pieces. To block your knitting, dampen the pieces, shape them to the finished dimensions usually by pinning them on a cloth covered board, and then let them dry in a warm dry place. You can also steam block your knitting with a steam iron held over the knitting as it is pulled into shape then left to cool. The steam method doesn't always have the same results as the dampening and pinning version, but it can be enough for some projects. Many of the projects in this book didn't need blocking, and those that did were steam set, rather than completely dampened and pinned in place. Sweaters, such as the Norwegian Ski Sweater on page 70, which features the natural curl of Stockinette stitch, should not be blocked along the curled edge.

Other Tools You May Need

In addition to yarn and needles, you will need
- Good lighting
- Scissors
- Tapestry needle (large with a blunt end) to weave in the ends of your yarn
- Tape measure to measure your gauge, knitting progress and the finished pieces

For some projects you may also need or want to have handy
- Stitch markers to mark increases, decreases and pattern changes
- Stitch holders to hold live stitches while working on another part of the project
- Row counters to keep track of the rows knitted
- Point protectors to keep stitches from falling off the needle when you aren't knitting
- Steam iron and/or large head pins for blocking finished pieces
- Crochet hooks of various sizes to pick up dropped stitches, to add fringe and to add
    finishing details, such as the Petit Smocked Bag on page 56
- Sewing machine for assembly of some projects

Embroidery and Embellishment Basics - *Embroidery and*
embellishment encompass a broad range of the needlearts with many nuances of technique and style. Following is a short coverage of the bare necessities you will need to get started if you have not done any embroidery or embellishment before. Seasoned needle artists will have their own methods and may only need this as a reference for the stitches. With that said, here are the techniques and methods that I used for the projects in this book beginning with how I begin and end my threads and yarns.

Beginnings and Endings - *Use the method on the left for yarn or thread that is almost as thick as your knitting yarn. Use the method on the right for all threads and yarns (beading or embroidery) thinner than your knitting yarn. For Swiss darning, use the "weave in ends" method on page 10.*

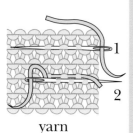

yarn

For Yarn - On the back side of the knitting, insert the needle where you want to begin, pass the needle through the knitting for about 1" (2.5 cm) (1), Pass back through the yarn to the beginning point (2) piercing the yarn in step 1 if possible to lock the yarn in place. Pass to the front of the knitting and begin embellishing, or cut the yarn if at the end of your work.

For Threads - On the back side of the knitting, insert the needle where you want to begin, pass the needle through the knitting for about 1" (2.5 cm) (1), take a small stitch in the knitting (2) and pull until there is a small loop of thread. Pass through the loop (3), then finish pulling the thread snuggly. Pass back through the yarn to the beginning point (4) and to the front of the knitting and begin embellishing, or cut the thread if at the end of your work.

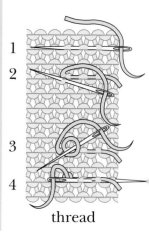

thread

Stitching on Knitted Fabric

Because knitted fabric is elastic, it's a little different to embroider on than woven fabric, and you have a few more things to consider before you begin. The first thing is the elasticity of knitting and how your embellishment will affect the project.

Most embroidery or embellishment techniques will make that portion of the knitting less elastic, or not elastic at all anymore. So it is a good idea to choose areas of the knitting that don't need to stretch when you wear them, or when you take them on and off. Sweaters should be loose fitting, and hats should fit the head without stretching too much. However, if the embellishments are isolated touches, such as in the Ocean Ermine scarf on page 33, or if you are working in a technique that is elastic in itself, such as Swiss darning, and you are careful to work diagonally or in a horizontal zigzag pattern when carrying thread on the backside of the work, then you don't have to worry because the elasticity of the knitting isn't affected, or will change only a little. The change in elasticity that occurs can be used to your advantage in some cases. Because embroidery and embellishments can stiffen the knitted fabric, they can help in forming the finished piece. The Crazy Quilt Stripes Bag on page 52 is sturdier along the embroidered section. Adding beads to edges of knitting can also help you to strengthen and define the knitted edges, such as on the Tunic Sweater Jacket on page 94, where the width of the bead pattern around the sleeve and neck edges, determines the finished size of those areas.

When you add embellishments such as beads you will usually need to pierce the knitted yarn to keep the beads on the front of the knitting. If the knitting is tight enough, though, and the beads are the same size as the stitches, or larger than the knitted stitches, you can sometimes add the beads by stitching around the knitted stitches with a tapestry needle, and the beads will stay in place, such as in the Little Black Bag on page 46. No matter what project you choose to embellish, take time to think about how the knitting will be used and how the embellishment will affect the finished structure of your project.

Threads

You can use just about any thread or cord for decorative embroidery. Some, like beading thread, are specific to their purpose, others like knitting yarn, are more versatile and can be used in several creative ways. Here are the types of fibers I used.

Beading thread - A thin, strong thread that can be made of synthetic material such as the Nymo brand shown, or natural fiber such as silk. Beading thread is used to make bead fringes and to sew beads to the knitted project.

Cotton cord - A twisted thread that comes in several sizes and many colors, used for decorative stitches.

Knitting yarn - This can be either the same yarn as was used for the knitted project, great for Swiss darning, or you can use a different type or size of yarn for bold embroidery stitches.

l. to r. - Nymo beading thread, size 12 variegated pearl cotton, size 8 pearl cotton, size 5 pearl cotton, sport weight knitting yarn

Needles

Each type of needle has it's own unique quality and use. Here are the indispensible tools I used for my stitching.

Tapestry needle - A blunt ended, large eyed, needle that is great for weaving in ends of yarn, sewing seams in knitted projects, and embroidery with yarn when the stitches pass around the knitting, rather than piercing the stitches.

Chenille needle - A sharp pointed, large eyed needle that is used for yarn and thick thread embroidery when you need to pierce the knitted stitches.

Beading needle - A needle that is thin enough to pass through bead holes. Bead embroidery needles are shorter and have a blunt end, while all other beading needles are longer and have a sharp point.

chenille needles

beading needles

tapestry needles

Beads

- Finding and choosing beads for a project is an adventure in itself. I encourage you to look for beads that you like and that go with the yarns you've chosen for your project, rather than trying to get the exact same beads that were used in the samples.

There is a multitude of bead shapes, colors and finishes to choose from so be sure to take your yarn with you to the bead store, and hold them up to each other so you can visualize the finished project. Beads can be round or square, short or long, have the hole passing through the middle or through one end (side drilled), or they can be symmetrical or pressed into shapes such as leaves, or faceted so they sparkle like diamonds. Here are some of the shapes of beads you might find when looking for the perfect embellishments for your project.

Keep in mind the following when choosing beads:

-delicate knitting can't carry the weight of a lot of heavy beads, so choose small beads for lightweight knitting.

-Bead holes vary in size, so make sure the beads you choose have holes big enough for your needle and thread.

-Some beads are unique, so be sure to purchase enough for your project, or ask if they are an item that is reorderable.

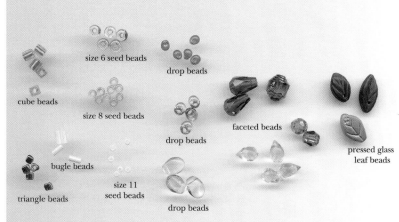

size 6 seed beads
drop beads
cube beads
size 8 seed beads
faceted beads
drop beads
pressed glass leaf beads
bugle beads
size 11 seed beads
triangle beads
drop beads

Attaching Beads to Knitting

- Always begin and end threads using the method on page 12. Always pierce the knitted stitches for each stitch so that the beads stay on the front of the knitted fabric, unless instructed otherwise, or when the knitting is tight enough to hold the beads on the front as described in Adding Beads over Knitted Stitches below.

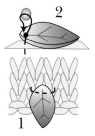

Attaching a Bead Dangle - *Can be added to the edge of knitting to make a fringe, or on the surface of the knitting for an accent.*

Attach the thread where you want the dangle to hang. String your chosen bead pattern, skip one or more of the last beads strung and pass the needle back up through the rest of the beads until you reach the knitting again. Before pulling the needle through the beads, slide the beads along the needle by pulling the needle toward you. This makes sure you haven't pierced the thread already in the beads. Now, hold on to the skipped beads with one hand and pull the thread through, (this helps to make sure you pull all the thread through evenly). Take a small stitch in the knitting and pull the thread almost all the way through so a small loop forms. Pass the needle through the loop then finish pulling the thread snuggly, so a small knot forms to lock the dangle in place.

Attaching Leaf Beads - *For leaf bead accents when you want individual leaves on the surface of the knitting.*

Come up from the back of the knitting and string a leaf bead. If the bead hole passes through the side of the bead, simply pass back down through the knitting, making a stitch the width of the bead (1). If the hole passes through the leaf from front to back, then string a small round bead such as a size 11 seed bead, and pass back down through the leaf bead and through the knitting in the same place where you originally came up through the knitting (2).

Looped Bead Edgings - *Worked either around the knitted stitches or through them with piercing.*

Begin with the thread coming out at the edge of the knitting. String a loop of beads. *Pass through the knitted edge enough stitches away to make the beads hang in a loop. Pass back through the last bead strung. String the same pattern of beads, less the first bead in the pattern, and repeat from asterisk.

Stitching Beads in a Line - *A form of backstitch.*

Come up from the back of the knitting, string about 3 to 5 beads. *Pass back down through the knitting, making the stitch the length of the group of beads. Pass back up through the knitting 1 or 2 bead widths back from the end of the stitch (1), and pass through 1 or 2 of the beads. String another group of beads (2), and repeat from asterisk.

Adding Beads over Knitted Stitches - *Beads need to be about the same size as one knitted stitch and the knitting needs to be firm. Pass over and under the knitted stitches rather than piercing them.*

*Come up from the back of the knitting to the right or left of the stitch to cover. String a bead, pass over the stitch to cover and back down to the back of the knitting, passing along the same row of knitting to the next stitch to cover with a bead. Repeat from asterisk.

14

Embroidery Stitches that Pierce the Knitted Stitch

- These stitches are sewn through the knitting as if it is a piece of fabric. They can be worked in any size thread, from thin decorative embroidery threads, to the yarn used to knit your project. Use a sharp needle, such as a chenille needle when working these stitches. Where you embroider in this technique, you will eliminate the stretch in the knitting, so keep that in mind when planning your design.

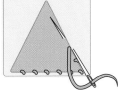

Blind Hem Stitch - *For applique.*
A functional stitch used in applique to sew the edges of a piece of fabric down to the base fabric. A very small stitch is made on the front of the piece through all thicknesses and then thread is carried along the backside a short distance. This is repeated around the applique.

Straight Stitch - *Can be short or long, in any direction.*
Come up where you want the stitch to begin, then pass down through the knitting where you want the stitch to end.

Stem Stitch - *Creates a line.*
Working from left to right, come up where you want the stitch to begin, and *back down about 2 knitted stitch lengths to the right, then back up 1 knitted stitch length to the left. Repeat from asterisk.

Back Stitch - *Creates a thin line.*
Working from right to left, come up 1 knitted stitch to the left of where you want the stitch to begin, and *back down 1 knitted stitch to the right. Come back up 2 knitted stitches to the left. Repeat from asterisk.

Satin Stitch - *Fills in shapes with color.*
Make straight stitches next to each other to fill in a shape with color.

Chain Stitch - *Same as Lazy Daisy, creates a thick line.*
Come up where you want the stitch to begin, then *insert the needle next to where the thread is coming out and exit about 1 or 2 knitted stitches away with the thread looped around the needle as shown above. Pull the thread until the loop forms around the exiting thread. Repeat from asterisk. To end the line, insert the needle just beyond the last loop to hold it in place as in step 2 for Filled Lazy Daisy Stitch.

Filled Lazy Daisy Stitch -
Often used for flower petals & leaves.
Make a single chain stitch (1), then tack the loop in place with a small stitch (2), then make a small straight stitch in the center of the loop (3).

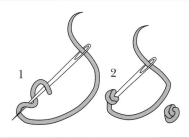

– straight stitch

French Knot - *Good for centers of flowers.*
Come up where you want the knot, wrap the thread around the needle 2 or 3 times (1). Insert the needle next to where you came up from the knitting, holding the thread so the wraps are snug, but not tight around the needle (2). Pull through to form the knot.

Fly Stitch - *Creates a "V" shape which can be isolated, or worked in a group to make a leaf shape as shown above on the right.*
*Come up at the top of the left leg of the "V" shape. Insert the needle where you want the top of the right leg of the "V" shape, and come out of the knitting where you want the base of the "V" shape, with the thread looped around the needle as shown (1). Pull through, then insert the needle again, just beyond the base of the "V" to hold the thread in place (2). Repeat from asterisk.

Embroidery Stitches that Pass Around the Knitted Stitch

These stitches, some of which are the same stitches as those on page 15, are worked on the knitting as if it's a piece of canvas in which each knitted stitch is an intersection of canvas. You will need to use a blunt tapestry needle so you can pass between and around the knitted stitches without piercing the yarn as you stitch. These stitches can be worked with yarn or with threads. Each will have a very different effect. Some of the stitches, such as chain stitch, will eliminate the stretch in the knitting, while others, like Swiss darning, will not. The only stitch not shown here is the smocking stitch used in the Petite Smocked bag. Detailed instructions for that stitch are shown on page 58 with the project instructions.

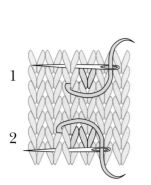
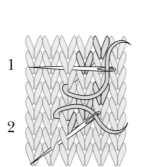
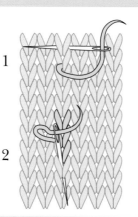
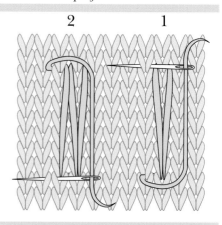

Swiss Darning - *The embroidery technique exclusive to knitting which mimics colorwork by stitching over finished knitting, following the stitch structure. Also called duplicate stitch.*

Working sideways, diagonally, or up and down, come up at the center of the base of the stitch to be covered. *Pass behind the next stitch above (1), insert the needle at the center of the base of the stitch where you first came up, exiting at the center of the base of the next stitch to cover (2). Repeat from asterisk.

Elongated Swiss Darning
- *A variation of Swiss darning.*
Work the same as the Swiss darning stitch except make each stitch over several rows of knitting, rather than just one stitch.

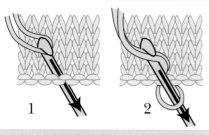

Attaching Yarn Fringe - *An easy edging to finish off a project.*
Cut yarn into strips twice as long as the finished fringe, plus about 1" (2.5 cm). Fold the length of yarn in half and hold in left hand. Slide crochet hook through edge stitch on knitting and grab fold of yarn you are holding. Pull through knitting (1). Wrap the ends of the yarn around the hook and pull through loop on hook (2). Pull tight, being careful not to tug on knitting. Repeat in each stitch along edge to make fringe. Trim ends of fringe so they are all the same length.

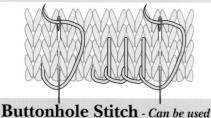

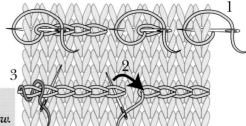

Buttonhole Stitch - *Can be used as an edging or decorative stitch.*
Make vertical stitches over one or more stitches, catching the thread behind the needle as shown above.

Lazy Daisy Stitch - *Called Chain Stitch when worked in a line as shown below.*
Work the same as Filled Lazy Daisy Stitch on page 15, working over 1 to 3 stitches of knitting and omitting the last straight stitch.

Whipped Chain Stitch
- *Colorful.*
Work a chain stitch along a row of knitting (1), finishing as shown in (2) above, if working in the round. With a different colored thread pass under each chain stitch, always in the same direction so the new thread makes diagonal lines over the chain stitches (3).

Half Cross Stitch - *small stitch.*
Make a diagonal stitch over one stitch as shown above. Can be worked in either direction.

Chain Stitch - *Eliminates stretch.*
Work the same as Chain Stitch on page 15, making each chain stitch over 1 or 2 knitted stitches.

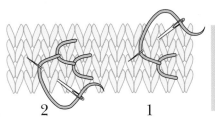

Feather Stitch - *Elastic stitch. Worked from right to left over 3 rows of knitting.*

Come up at the bottom row, *insert the needle up one row, coming out one stitch to the left and between the 2 rows, looping the yarn around the needle as shown (1). Pull through. Repeat once from asterisk, then change direction for each stitch as shown in (2).

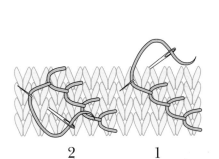

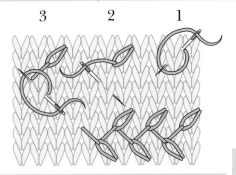

Double Feather Stitch - *Creates a beautiful elastic stitch.*

Work the same as Feather Stitch, except make several stitches in one direction (1), then change direction (2) making the same number of stitches in the opposite direction. Repeat across.

Feathered Chain Stitch - *An elastic stitch that resembles a vine of leaves. Working from right to left, over 3 rows of knitting.*

Make a chain stitch diagonally over 1 stitch (1), make a straight stitch diagonally over 1 stitch, coming out 1 stitch diagonally down to the right (2). Repeat the process in the opposite diagonal direction (3), then alternate direction for each repeat.

Cretan Stitch - *Elastic from side to side only. Worked from left to right with knitting sideways, over 3 columns of knitting.*

Begin by coming out above the first column. Insert the needle behind the next stitch to the right in the top column, from top to bottom, catching the yarn under the needle as shown (1). Insert the needle in the next stitch to the right in the bottom column, from bottom to top, catching the yarn under the needle as shown (2). Repeat from asterisk.

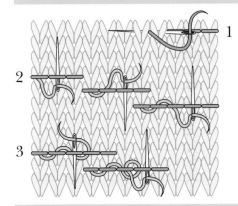

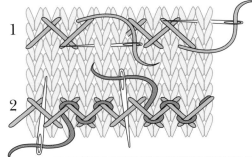

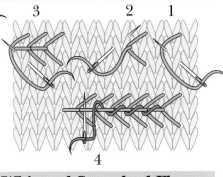

Threaded Back Stitch Variation - *Easier than it sounds. Be sure to pull the second stitching thread loosely into place so the loops and waves don't disappear. Not elastic. Worked over 1 row of knitting.*

Make a row of back stitches as on pg. 15, working each back stitch over 1 knitted stitch (1). With a new color of thread, working from left to right, *pass under each back stitch, first from bottom to top, then top to bottom, then bottom to top (2). For the decorative loop, pass from top to bottom behind 1 back stitch to left, then bottom to top through next back stitch to right. (3). Repeat steps 2 and 3, reversing direction you pass through back stitches: top to bottom, then bottom to top, top to bottom, then make loop bottom to top through one back stitch to the left, ending top to bottom next back stitch to right. Repeat from asterisk.

Threaded Herring-bone Stitch - *A colorful, elastic stitch. Worked over 3 rows of knitting.*

For Herringbone stitch, work from left to right. Begin with the thread coming out of the first stitch on the bottom row. *Pass behind the next stitch to the right on the top row from right to left. Pass behind the next stitch to the right on the bottom row from right to left. Repeat from asterisk (1). With a new color of thread, working from right to left, begin with the thread coming out of the top row. **Pass down under the first herringbone stitch to the left. Pass up under the next (2). Repeat from double asterisks.

Whipped Stretched Fly Stitch - *A lacy, elastic stitch. Worked from right to left over 3 rows of knitting.*

Begin with the thread coming out of the top row on the right. Insert the needle into the same place 2 rows down, exiting 1 stitch up and to the left, catching the thread behind the needle as shown (1). *Insert the needle 1 stitch to the left, exiting 1 stitch up and to the right (2). Insert the needle 2 stitches down, exiting 1 stitch up and to the left, catching the thread behind the needle as shown (3) Repeat from asterisk. With a new color of thread, begin at the center horizontal stitch and pass under each horizontal stitch always passing in the same direction, creating diagonal lines of color (4).

17

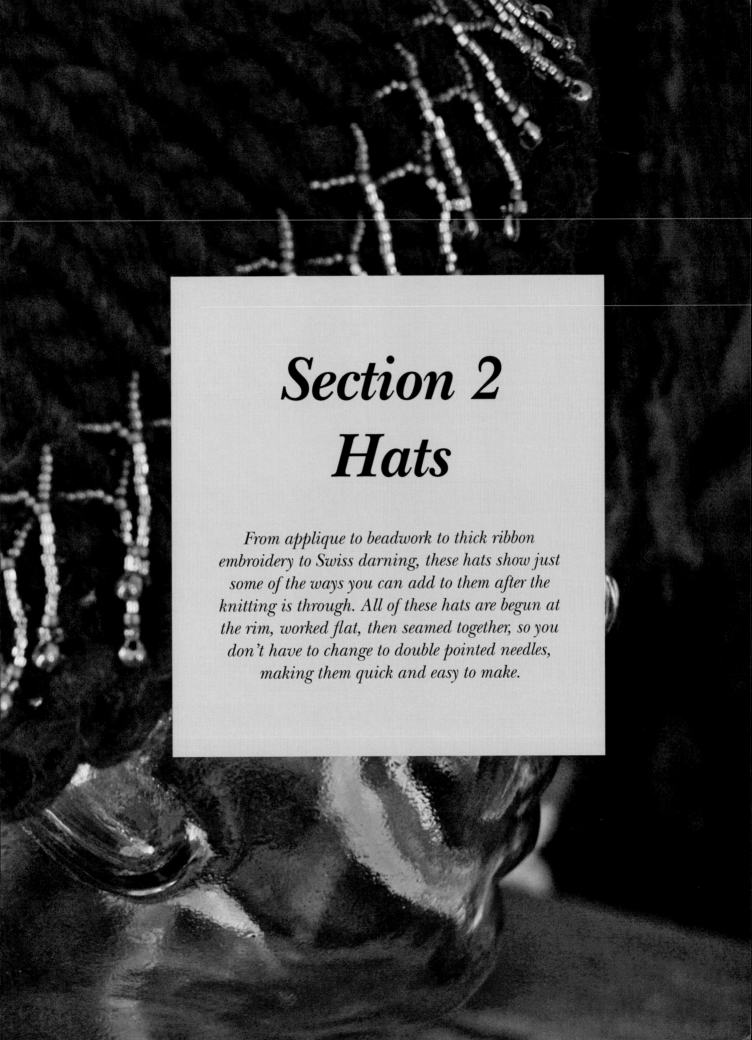

Section 2
Hats

From applique to beadwork to thick ribbon embroidery to Swiss darning, these hats show just some of the ways you can add to them after the knitting is through. All of these hats are begun at the rim, worked flat, then seamed together, so you don't have to change to double pointed needles, making them quick and easy to make.

Big Yarn Beaded Hats

You can knit these hats in an afternoon and wear them as is, or add a little sparkle with the simple green hat bead edging, or the dangly fringe on the plum hat. The roving yarn and large needles make these hats quick to knit and the yarn is soft, thick and comfortable. Adding the beadwork gives these hats your creative touch.

Finished size
To fit 22" (55 cm) circumference head

Materials
1 hank (3.5oz/100g, 45yd/42m) super bulky roving wool yarn (6)
Size 17 (12.75 mm) knitting needles at least 14" (35 mm) long
Tapestry needle
Beading needle and thread to match yarn color
Green Hat Beads
    35 4mm round beads
    70 size 11 medium green seed beads
    140 size 11 lime green seed beads
    70 size 8 muted green seed beads
Purple Hat Beads
    70 size 5 magenta drop beads
    140 size 8 magenta triangle beads
    140 size 8 dark purple seed beads
    700 size 11 light silver lined pink beads
    840 size 11 purple beads
Note: bead quantities will be less if you make a thick seam.

This project was made using the following yarns
Blue Sky Alpacas Bulky Hand Dyes (50% alpaca/50% wool, 3.5oz/100g, 45yd/42m) 1 hank in color #1017 granny smith for green hat, and 1 hank in color #1014 purple for plum hat.

Gauge in Stockinette Stitch
7 sts and 11 rows = 4" (10 cm)

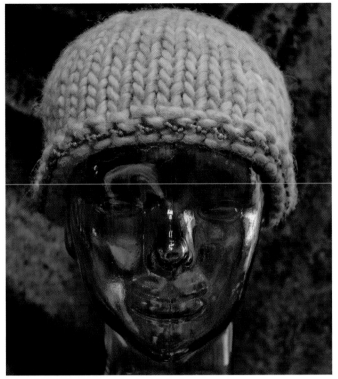

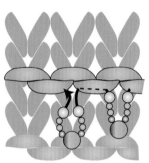

- ⊙ size 11 medium green seed bead
- ⊙ size 11 lime green seed bead
- ○ size 8 muted green seed bead
- ⬭ 4mm round bead

Hat (Worked flat, then seamed together)
CO 35 sts.
Row 1 – 3: Knit.
Row 4: Purl.
Row 5: Knit.
Row 6: Purl.
Rows 7 – 12: Continue in Stockinette stitch.
Row 13: (K2tog, k3) rep 7 times – 28 sts.
Row 14: Purl.
Row 15: (K2tog, k2) rep 7 times – 21 sts.
Row 16: Purl.
Row 17: (K2tog, k1) rep 7 times – 14 sts.
Row 18: Purl.
Row 19: K2tog rep 7 times – 7 sts.
Cut the working yarn to 18" (45 cm) and thread with a tapestry needle. Pass through remaining sts. Sew seam using mattress stitch. Weave in ends. No need to block.

Embroidery

Green Hat

Attach the beading thread along the bottom of the second garter stitch ridge. *String the beads as shown at left and pass through the next stitch on the hat. Repeat from asterisk all the way around the hat. Weave in ends.

Purple Hat

Attach the beading thread along the 4th row of knitting above the garter stitch rows. *String the beads to the end of the first arrow shown below (1), skip the last three beads strung and pass the needle back through all the beads except for the first 6 purple beads. String 6 more purple beads (2) and pass through half of the next stitch on the hat as shown. Repeat from asterisk in every stitch along the row (A). Stitch the same pattern on the 5th row, offsetting the pattern by half of a knitted stitch (B). Weave in ends.

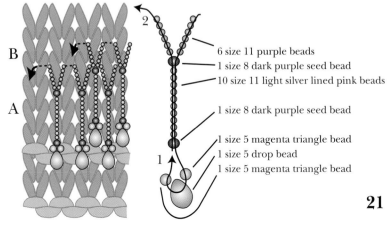

- 6 size 11 purple beads
- 1 size 8 dark purple seed bead
- 10 size 11 light silver lined pink beads
- 1 size 8 dark purple seed bead
- 1 size 5 magenta triangle bead
- 1 size 5 drop bead
- 1 size 5 magenta triangle bead

21

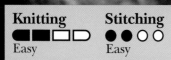
Triangles Hat

Dress up a plain, easy hat with some colorful triangles that change color as you knit them with the variegated yarn. Be sure to make the hat so it fits your head without stretching much, or your stitched triangles will pull against the knitting as it stretches to fit.

Finished size
To fit 22" (55 cm) circumference head

Materials
1 skein (4oz/113g, 190yd/173m) burgundy worsted weight
    yarn 🧶4
Less than 1 skein (.25oz/7g, 31yd/28m) variegated reds
    sock weight yarn 🧶1
Size 9 (5.5 mm) 24" (60 cm) circular knitting needles
Size 2 (2.75 mm) knitting needles at least 6" (15 cm) long
Tapestry needle

This project was made using the following yarn
1 skein Brown Sheep's Lamb's Pride worsted weight yarn
(85% wool/15% mohair, 4oz/113g, 190yd/173m) color
M-185 Aubergine (burgundy) and 1 skein Brown Sheep's
Handpaint Wildfoote Luxury Sock Yarn (75% washable
wool/25% nylon, 1.75oz/50g, 215yd/197m) color SY-300
Ragtime (variegated reds).

**Gauge in Stockinette Stitch using the larger needles and
    yarn**
17.5 sts and 22 rows = 4" (10 cm)

Hat (Worked flat, then seamed together)
Using larger needles and worsted weight yarn, CO 88 sts.
Work in St st for 40 rows.
Row 41: (K2tog, k 9) rep 8 times – 80 sts.
Row 42 and all even rows: Purl.
Row 43: (K2tog, k8) rep 8 times – 72 sts.
Row 45: (K2tog, k7) rep 8 times – 64 sts.
Continue decrease pattern until there are 16 sts left.
Cut yarn to 18" (45 cm), thread with tapestry needle and
pass through remaining sts.
Sew seam using mattress stitch, weave in ends. Do not
block. Let rim curl up naturally.

Triangles (make about 9 large and 6 small triangles)
Using smaller needles and sock weight yarn, CO 16 sts for large triangle or 10 sts for small triangle.
Row 1: Knit.
Row 2 and all even rows: Purl.
Row 3: K2tog through back of sts, k to last 2 sts, k2tog – large triangle 14 sts, small triangle 8 sts.
Repeat row 3 for all right side rows until 2 sts remain. On next right side row k2tog, cut yarn to 12" (30 cm) and pull through remaining loop. Steam press all triangles flat.

Embroidery

Using the tails on the triangles, sew triangles to the hat, randomly spaced just above the curled rim as shown in photo.

Blind Hem Stitch
Beginning with the yarn coming out through the edge of the triangle, take a small stitch in the hat, bringing the needle up through the hat and the edge of the triangle about 1/4" (.5 cm) away. Pull the yarn so that the stitches barely show. Repeat around the triangle.

Sparkling Leaves Spring Hat

Using large needles and holding three strands of beautiful yarn together as one allows you to knit this sparkly hat in no time. Then you can embellish it with a special accent bead and embroider leaves in lazy daisy stitch with thick ribbon. You only use a little of the ribbon so you could easily make the coordinating scarf on page 30.

Finished size
To fit 22" (55 cm) circumference head

Materials
1 ball (1.75oz/50g, 154yd/140m), emerald/green/yellow sport weight mohair blend (**2**)

1 ball (.9oz/25g, 124yd/112m), navy/brown angora blend (**2**)

1 ball (1.75oz/50g, 127yd/116m), moss green 1/8" nylon tape (**3**)

Less than 1 yd mint/sky green 9/16" (1.25 cm) wide ribbon (**5**)

Size 10.5 (6.5 mm) 24" (60 cm) circular knitting needles

Tapestry needle

1" (2.4 cm) accent bead

4 g size 8 mint green seed beads

8 size 5 green seed beads

8 side drilled oblong pale green pearls

Beading needle and beading thread to match yarn or beads

This project was made using the following yarn
One ball each of Louisa Harding Impression (84% nylon/16% mohair, 1.75oz/50g, 154yd/140m) color #4 Emerald/green/yellow, Kimono Angora (70% angora, 25% wool, 5% nylon, .65oz/25g, 124yd/112m) color #8 Navy/brown, Fauve (100% nylon, 1.75oz/50g, 127yd/116m) color #6 moss green, Sari Ribbon (90% nylon/10% metallic, 1.75oz/50g, 66yd/60m) color #2 mint/sky green

Gauge in Stockinette Stitch
14 sts and 19 rows = 4" (10 cm)

Hat (Worked flat, then seamed together)
Holding 3 of the different yarns together as one, not including the 9/16" (1.5 cm) wide ribbon, CO 72 sts.
Row 1: Knit.
Row 2: Purl.
Row 3 and 4: (K1, p1) rep across.
Row 5 and 6: (P1, k1) rep across.
Row 7: Knit.
Row 8: Purl.
Row 9 – 24: Continue in Stockinette stitch.
Row 25: (K2tog, k7) repeat 8 times – 64 sts.
Row 27: (K2tog, k6) repeat 8 times – 56 sts.
Row 29: (K2tog, k5) repeat 8 times – 48 sts.
Continue in decrease pattern until there are 16 sts left. Cut yarn to 18" (45 cm), thread with tapestry needle, pass through remaining sts, and sew seam closed using mattress stitch. Weave in ends. No need to block.

Embroidery
Using the beading thread and needle, sew the accent bead to the hat approx 2"(5 cm) from the bottom edge and about 3" (7.5 cm) to the right of center. Using the thick ribbon and tapestry needle stitch lazy daisy stitches radiating out from the accent bead.
Stitch straight stitches of beads radiating out from the accent bead, stringing several size 8 beads, one pearl, one size 5 bead and one size 8 bead. Stitch several dangles below and to the side of the accent bead as shown. Weave in ends.

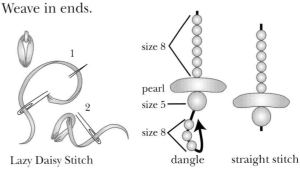

Lazy Daisy Stitch   dangle   straight stitch **25**

Easy Falling Snow Hat

Hats are great projects to embroider since they are so quick and small. This warm hat knits up quickly with the ribbing made on large needles, holding two strands of yarn together as one. If you don't want to double fold the ribbing, you can make it 6" (15 cm) long instead of 8" (20 cm) for a classic ribbed hat.

Finished size
To fit 22" (55 cm) circumference head

Materials
1 1/2 skeins (3.5oz/100g, 245yd/226m each) of dark blue worsted
 weight yarn ④
Less than 3 yds of white worsted weight yarn ④
Size 7 (4.5 mm) 24" (60 cm) circular knitting needles
Size 10 1/2 (6.5 mm) 24" (60 cm) circular knitting needles
Stitch markers
Tapestry needle

This project was made using the following yarn
Harrisville Designs The Orchid Line (70% fine pure wool/25% mohair/5% silk, 3.5oz/100g, 245yd/226m) two skeins in color #234 "Night Skies" and one skein in color #226 "White Orchid"

Gauge in Stockinette Stitch using the smaller needles and one strand of yarn
18 sts and 20 rows = 4" (10 cm)

Hat (Worked flat, then seamed together)
Holding 2 strands of the dark blue yarn together as one, and using the larger size needles, CO 60 sts.
Work in k1, p1 rib for 8" (20 cm).
Change to the smaller needles, one strand of yarn, and separate each stitch into two strands of yarn as you work, (k8, k2tog) repeat 12 times - 108 sts. Purl the next row.
Work 8 more rows in Stockinette stitch.
On the next row (k2tog, k10, place marker) repeat across - 99 sts. Purl the next row.
Work 2 more rows in Stockinette stitch.
Continuing in Stockinette stitch, dec 1 st at each marker on every right side row until you have 18 sts left (9 sts decreased each right side row).

Cut the yarn to 18" (45 cm), thread with a tapestry needle, pass through remaining sts and sew side seam using mattress stitch. No need to block. Turn ribbing up about 5" (12.5 cm), then down about 3" (7.5 cm) to make a thick double folded rib.

Embroidery
Using the white yarn and tapestry needle, begin near the center top of the hat and make single stitches in Swiss darning, about 1" (2.5 cm) apart randomly on the hat.

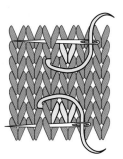

Swiss darning stitch

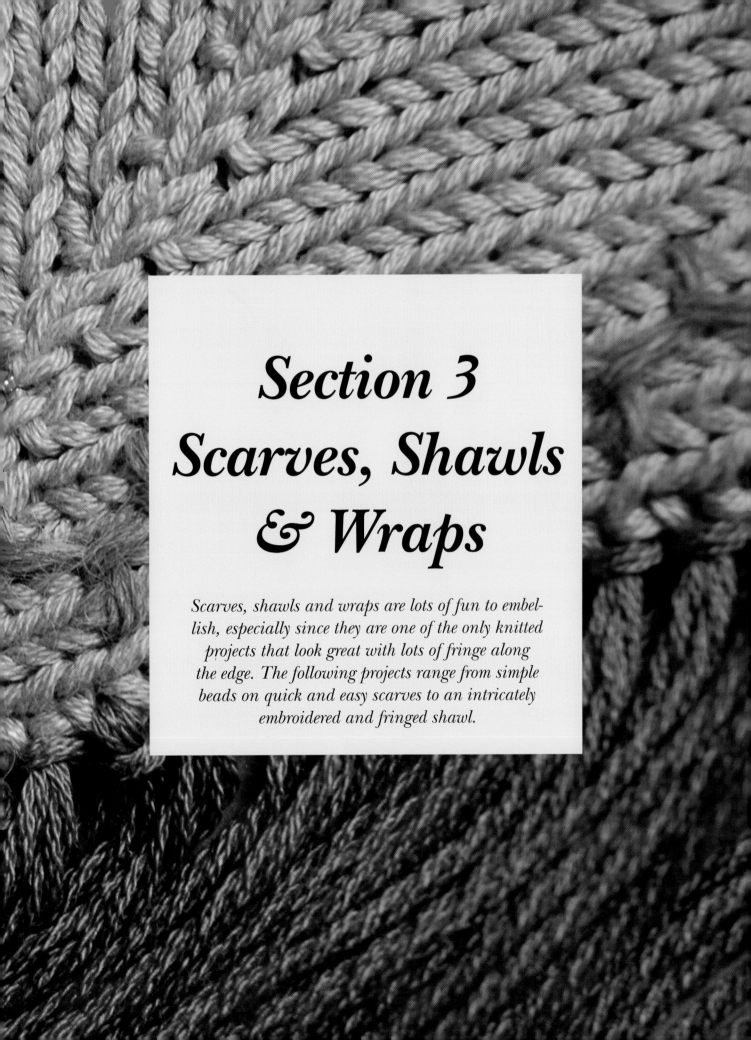

Section 3
Scarves, Shawls
& Wraps

Scarves, shawls and wraps are lots of fun to embellish, especially since they are one of the only knitted projects that look great with lots of fringe along the edge. The following projects range from simple beads on quick and easy scarves to an intricately embroidered and fringed shawl.

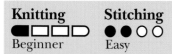
Ribbon Scarf

Beautiful knitting ribbon and large needles are all you need to whip up an elegant garter stitched scarf in an afternoon. Adding a beaded fringe to the ends creates a sparkly detail that sets this scarf apart from the rest.

Finished size

3 1/2" (9 cm) wide by 52" (130 cm) long, not including bead fringe

Materials

1 skein (1.75oz/50g, 66yd/60m) of mint/sky green 9/16" (1.25 cm) wide ribbon **⑤**
Size 13 (9 mm) knitting needles at least 7" long
Approx. 4 g size 11 pale green seed beads
Approx. 28 g size 8 pale green seed beads
Approx. 48 pink drop beads
Approx. 48 size 5 pink cube beads
Beading needle and beading thread to match ribbon color

This project was made using the following yarn

One skein Louisa Harding Sari Ribbon (90% nylon/10% metallic, 1.75oz/50g, 66yd/60m) color #2 mint/sky

Gauge in Stockinette Stitch

14 sts and 8 rows = 4" (10 cm)

Scarf

CO 12 sts. Work in Garter stitch, knitting until the scarf is about 52" long, or until you have just enough yarn to BO, BO.
Weave in ends. Steam scarf, holding iron above the knitting and pulling the scarf gently to lengthen and narrow it to the finished dimensions.

Beaded Fringe

Attach the thread to the first stitch at one end of the scarf. *String 20 size 8 seed beads, one size 5 cube bead, two size 11 seed beads, one drop bead, and two more size 11 seed beads. Pass the needle back through the cube bead and all the size 8 seed beads. Make a small stitch in the ribbon and pass the needle through the loop that forms as you pull the thread through. This will lock the dangle in place. Pass the needle through the ribbon about 1/4" (.5 cm) away. Repeat from asterisk for each dangle to make the fringe all the way across the edge of the scarf. Make the same fringe at the other end of the scarf.

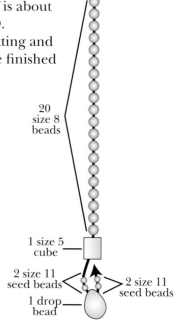

scarf

20
size 8
beads

1 size 5
cube

2 size 11
seed beads

2 size 11
seed beads

1 drop
bead

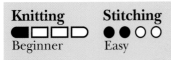
Ocean Ermine Scarf

Ermine, the white fur with black spots used to line the coats of royalty, inspired this eyelash scarf with it's sparkly dangles of faceted beads peeking through the lower edges of the scarf.

Finished size

52" (130 cm) long by approx. 3" (7.5 cm) wide, increasing to approx. 5" (12.5 cm) wide at ends

Materials

1 ball (1.75oz/50g, 66yd/61m) of novelty eyelash yarn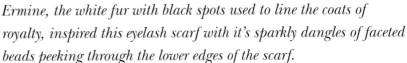
Size 17 (12 mm) knitting needles at least 7" (17.5 cm) long
Approx. 30 turquoise 1/2" (1 cm) long faceted drop beads
Approx. 30 turquoise 1/4" wide spacer beads
Less than 4 g size 11 blue/purple seed beads
Less than 4 g size 8 blue/purple seed beads
Beading thread to match yarn color
Beading needle
Tapestry needle

This project was made using the following yarn

Trendsetter Yarns' Coconut (100% polyamide, 1.75oz/50g, 66yd/61m) 1 ball in color #12

Gauge in Stockinette Stitch

18 1/2 sts and 10 rows = 4" (10 cm)

Scarf

CO 14 sts.
Work in Garter stitch until you have just enough yarn to BO, BO.
Weave in ends. Do not block.

Embroidery

Using the beading thread and needle, string ten size 11 seed beads, one size 8 seed bead, one spacer bead, one faceted drop bead and three size 11 seed beads. Skip the last three beads strung, and pass back through all the other beads so you have the tail and working thread coming out through the first bead strung. Pass the needle under one of the stitches on the scarf and tie both ends of thread into a square knot. Pass each end of thread back down through seven or eight beads in the dangle and cut the thread close to the beads. Make about 15 dangles randomly spaced about 1" (2.5 cm) apart on the lower edges of the scarf.

Knitting

■■□□
Easy

Stitching

●●○○
Easy
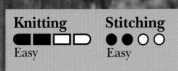

Woodland Scarf

This woodsy style scarf with it's beautiful heathered yarn is the perfect backdrop for leaf shaped beads with little "branches". Turning the long edges of the scarf over to the front adds texture to the design.

Finished size
9 1/2" (24 cm) wide by 54" (135 cm) long

Materials
2 skeins (3.5oz/100g, 132yd/122m) heather green
  worsted weight yarn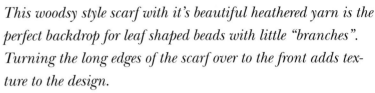
Size 9 (5.5 mm) knitting needles at least 10" long
Tapestry needle
Approx. 4 g size 11 bronze colored seed beads
Approx. 60 half inch long leaf shaped beads
Beading needle and beading thread in color to match yarn

This project was made using the following yarn
Cascade's Pastaza (50% llama/50% wool, 3.5oz/100g, 132yd/122m) 2 skeins in color #66 heather green

Gauge in Stockinette Stitch
16 sts and 20 rows = 4" (10 cm)

Scarf
CO 42 sts. Work in Stockinette stitch until piece measures 54" (135 cm) long, BO, block to 10 1/2" (26 cm) wide.

Finishing
Fold long edges of scarf over from the back to the front along the 4th stitch from the edge and stitch in place with a blind hem stitch.

Embroidery
Using the beading needle and thread, sew the leaves randomly to the last 6" (15 cm) of the scarf ends. Sew straight stitches of the smaller beads to represent stems of the leaf beads. If the leaf bead holes go through the side of the bead, stitch them in place with a straight stitch. If the leaf bead holes go through the bead from front to back, string the leaf bead and one small bead, then pass back down through the leaf bead so the small bead and the thread hold the leaf in place.

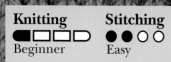
Black Swirls Wrap

This plain Stockinette stitch rectangle is spruced up with a narrow band of Swiss darned swirls and matching black fringe. Making it a wide 25" (62.5 cm) offsets the slight curl that naturally happens on the edges of Stockinette stitch projects.

Finished size

25" (62.5 cm) by 50" (125 cm), not including 7" (17.5 cm) fringe

Materials

4 skeins (3.5oz/100g, 136yd/126m) of teal heavy worsted weight yarn (5)
2 skeins (3.5oz/100g, 136yd/136m) of black heavy worsted weight yarn (5)
Size 10 (6 mm) 24" (60 cm) long circular knitting needles
Size H crochet hook to attach fringe
Tapestry needle

This project was made using the following yarn

Berroco's Softwist Bulky (59% rayon/41% wool, 3.5oz/100g, 136yd/126m) four 4 skeins in color #7479 "Turquoise" and two skeins in color #7434 "Pitch Black"

Gauge in Stockinette Stitch

14 1/2 sts and 22 rows = 4" (10 cm)

Scarf

Using the teal colored yarn, CO 90 sts.
Work in Stockinette stitch until the scarf is 50" (125 cm) long, BO. Weave in ends. Block.

Embroidery

Using a 24" (60 cm) length of the black yarn and the tapestry needle, stitch the black swirl pattern along both edges of the scarf, beginning on the 12th row from the ends.

Fringe

Cut 180 15" (37.5 cm) strips of black yarn. Fold one in half and attach to the first stitch at one corner of the scarf with the crochet hook as shown. Repeat for each knitted stitch along both ends of the scarf.

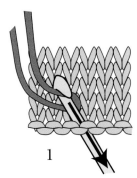

Attaching Fringe

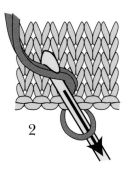

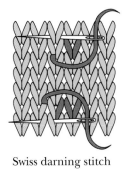

Swiss darning stitch

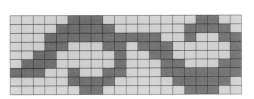

Black Swirls chart

37

Celtic Diamonds Scarf

This soft, thick, hand dyed yarn is a delight to work with, knitting up quickly and showing off the seed stitch border. The bold Swiss darned pattern is ideal for this technique, since if you follow along the diagonal lines of the pattern as you stitch, the back of the scarf has a clean, finished look.

Finished size
8 1/4" (20.5 cm) wide by 60" (150 cm) long

Materials
3 skeins (3.5oz/100g, 100yd/92m) of purple heavy worsted weight yarn 5
Less than 1 skein (3.5oz/100g, 100yd/92m) of ecru heavy worsted weight yarn 5
Size 10 (6 mm) knitting needles at least 10" long
Tapestry needle

This project was made using the following yarn
Blue Sky Alpacas' Worsted Hand Dyes (50% alpaca/50% merino, 3.5oz/100g, 100yd/92m) 3 skeins in color #2004 "Purple" and one skein in color #2003 "Ecru"

Gauge in Stockinette Stitch
17 sts and 21 rows = 4" (10 cm)

Scarf
Using the purple yarn, CO 35 sts.
Row 1: (K1, p1) rep twice, k to last 4 sts, (p1, k1) rep twice.
Row 2: (K1, p1) rep twice, p to last 4 sts, (p1, k1) rep twice.
Rep row 1 and row 2 until you have just enough yarn to BO.
BO, weave in ends. Block.

Swiss Darning
Using a 24" (60 cm) length of the ecru yarn and the tapestry needle, stitch the diamond pattern along one end of the scarf, beginning the point of the first large diamond in the center stitch of the first row of the scarf. Follow the chart to the center row, then reverse direction creating a mirror image of the chart. Weave in the ends on the back of the scarf, following the ecru colored yarn already showing, so the wrong side looks as neat at the front. Repeat the pattern at the other end of the scarf.

center row

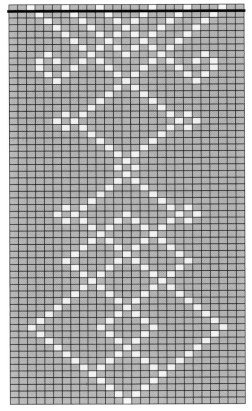

Celtic Diamonds Chart

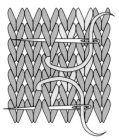

Swiss darning stitch

Meandering Vine Shawl

This large, plain and easy to knit Egyptian cotton shawl transforms into a beauty when you embroider it with a flowering vine, using the wonderful soft colors of alpaca yarn. Adding the long fringe and cretan stitch border adds to the details which are finished off with a small bead accent at the tip of the shawl.

Finished size
66" (165 cm) wide by 45" (112.5 cm) long at center point

Materials
4 skeins (4.5oz/125g, 256yd/236m) blue dk weight yarn
2 skeins (4.5oz/125g, 256yd/236m) pale turquoise dk weight yarn
1 skein ea (1.75oz/50g, 109yd/101m) sport weight yarn in green, yellow green, cream, wheat, and lavender
Size 5 (3.75 mm) 32" (80 cm) circular knitting needles
Tapestry needle
1 ball size 8 pearl cotton in green
About 20 beads in a variety of sizes and types for an accent dangle. The beads I used are listed on page 43
Beading needle and thread to match beads

This project was made using the following yarn and embroidery thread
Classic Elite's Provence (100% mercerized Egyptian cotton, 4.5oz/125g, 256yd/236m) three in color #2648 "Slate Blue" (blue), two in color #2621 "Herbal Sage" (pale turquoise) and Classic Elite's Inca Alpaca (100% alpaca, 1.75oz/50g, 109yds/101m) one skein each in colors #1135 "Cala Cala Moss" (green), #1131 "Blue Danube" (lavender), #1116 "Natural" (cream), #1117 "Gold Finch" (wheat), # 1197 "Canyon Green" (yellow green)
DMC's size 8 pearl cotton (100% cotton, 10g, 80m) in color #3345 "Dark Hunter Green"

Gauge in Stockinette Stitch
20 sts and 28 rows = 4" (10 cm)

Notes:
Inc on knit row: knit into front and back of st.
Inc on purl row: purl into front and back of st.

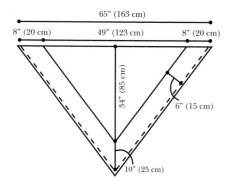

Large blue triangle.

Using the blue yarn, CO 3 sts.
Row 1: Knit.
Row 2: Purl.
Row 3: Inc 1, k across - 4 sts.
Row 4: Inc 1, p across - 5 sts.
Repeat row 3 and row 4 until there are 245 sts. BO, weave in ends. Block.

Border Strips

Right Side Strip:
Using the pale turquoise yarn, CO 3 sts.
Row 1: Knit.
Row 2: Purl.
Row 3: Knit.
Row 4: Inc 1, p across - 4 sts.
Repeat row 3 and row 4 until there are 36 sts.
Work even in St st until shorter section of piece meas the same as the right side of the blue triangle.
Cont in St st, dec 1 st at the end of ea right side row and the beg of ea wrong side row, rep until there are 3 sts left. Cut yarn and pass through rem sts. Weave in ends. Block.

Left Side Strip:
Using the pale turquoise yarn, CO 3 sts.
Row 1: Knit.
Row 2: Purl.
Row 3: Inc 1, k across - 4 sts.
Row 4: Purl.
Repeat row 3 and row 4 until there are 36 sts.
Work even in St st until shorter section of piece meas the same as the left side of the blue triangle.
Cont in St st, dec 1 st at the beg of ea right side row and the end of ea wrong side row, rep until there are 3 sts left. Cut yarn and pass through rem sts. Weave in ends. Block.

Assembly

Sew tog as shown at left using mattress stitch. Fold border edges under 6 sts and sew in place along every other row on the back of the shawl. Using the blue yarn, pick up and knit every st along the top of the right border, 4 sts for every 5 sts along the top edge of the blue section, and every st along the top of the left border - 256 sts. Work 2 rows in garter stitch, 2 rows in seed stitch, purl the next 2 rows, then BO. Steam block seams.

Transfering the Embroidery design

Following the diagram at right, trace the main vine pattern onto a piece of paper. Cut out the vine lines, so you have a thin opening showing the pattern. Place the pattern along one side of the border, near the point of the shawl, using the photo on page 41 as a guide, with the pattern lining up about 1" (2.5 cm) from the blue section of knitting. Using a contrasting thread, sew long stitches along the vine lines on the border knitting (these will be removed later). Reposition the paper along the border and continue sewing the pattern until you have the vine basted along one side of the shawl border. Flip the pattern and repeat on the border along the other side of the shawl.

Embroidery

Using the diagram at right, the illustrations below, and the detailed stitch instructions on page 15, stitch the embroidery pattern on the shawl, removing the vine basting thread as you sew. Use the pearl cotton for the chain stitched vine and leaf stems and the alpaca yarn for all the other embroidery.

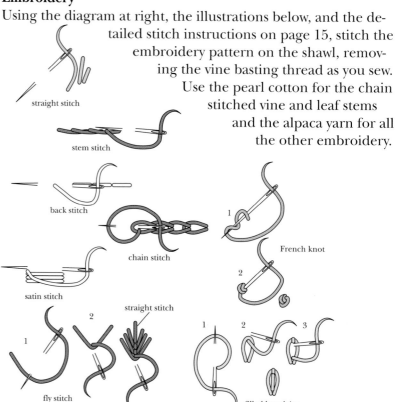

Stitch a row of Cretan stitch using the lavender alpaca yarn, one stitch in from the edge of the borders. The stitch is worked from right to left with the knitting sideways, over 3 columns of knitting. Begin by coming out above the first column. *Insert the needle behind the stitch 2 stitches to the right in the top column, from top to bottom, catching the yarn under the needle as shown (1). Insert the needle in stitch 2 stitches to the right in the bottom column, from bottom to top, catching the yarn under the needle as shown (2). Repeat from asterisk.

Fringe

Cut 340 15" lengths of the blue yarn. Attach to the border edges of the shawl following **Attaching Yarn Fringe** on page 16, attaching one strand of yarn to every other stitch along the edge. Cut more strands of yarn, if necessary.

Bead Dangle

Choose your own beads or the following beads that I used for my dangle:
9 size 11 seed beads
5 - 1/4" (5 mm) wide spacer beads
2 - 4 mm Swarovski crystals
1 - 3/16" long faceted drop bead
1 - 1/4" (5 mm) faceted round bead

String the beads you have chosen for your dangle, skipping the beads that will hang at the end of the dangle and passing back up through the rest of the beads so both threads are coming out of the top end of the dangle. Place the dangle on the shawl so the end lies just a little beyond the edge. Sew in place on the shawl with the remaining beading thread and needle. You can let the dangle hang freely from it's top, or tack it down a little closer to the edge of the shawl as well, so it stays at the center of the point of the shawl. Weave in ends.

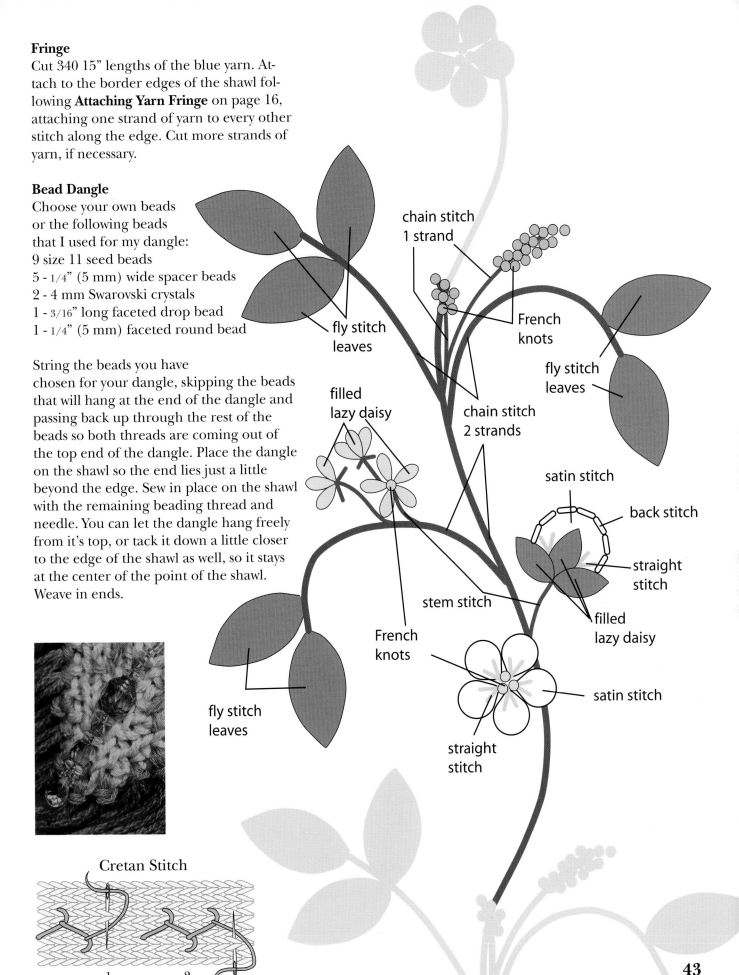

chain stitch
1 strand

French knots

fly stitch leaves

fly stitch leaves

filled lazy daisy

chain stitch 2 strands

satin stitch

back stitch

straight stitch

filled lazy daisy

stem stitch

French knots

fly stitch leaves

satin stitch

straight stitch

Cretan Stitch

1   2

43

Section 4
Purses & Bags

These four bags present four very different looks, exploring four different embellishment techniques, from beadwork to embroidery to three dimensional appliqué to smocking.

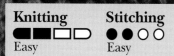

Little Black Purse

Beads are easy to stitch on this small cotton bag, since each knitted stitch is just about the same size as one bead. This technique can be used with cross stitch or needlepoint charts to create an intricate picture in beads. Your finished knitting needs to have a fairly tight tension to keep the beads in place on the front of the knitting.

Finished size
5 3/4" (14.5 cm) wide by 7 1/2" (19.5 cm) tall with a
   34" (85 cm) strap

Materials
1 skein (1.75oz/50g, 74yd/68m) of black dk weight
   cotton yarn
Size 5 (3.75 mm) knitting needles at least 10" (25 cm)long
Tapestry needle thin enough to string size 6 beads
36 size 6 purple seed beads
One 1/2" long accent bead
One 1/4" drop bead
Beading needle and black beading thread
Size 8 black pearl cotton

This project was made using the following yarn
Tahki Yarns' Cotton Classic II (100% mercerized cotton, 1.75oz/
50g, 74yd/68m) color #2002 black

Gauge in Stockinette Stitch
19 sts and 27 rows = 4" (10 cm)

Bag
CO 30 sts.
Work in Stockinette stitch until piece measures 15" (37.5) long.
On the next right side row, slip 1 stitch, knit two together as one, knit to the last 3 sts, knit two together as one, slip the last stitch.
Purl all wrong side rows.
Work the above two rows until you have 2 stitches left.
Cut yarn to 4" (10 cm) and pass through stitches.
Weave in ends.
Fold the cast on edge up 7" (27.5 cm) and sew side seams in mattress stitch.
Make 34" (85 cm) long 3-st I-cord.
Sew to top corners of bag.

Embroidery

Using the beading thread and needle, attach the thread to the tip of the flap, string the accent bead and drop bead then pass back through the accent bead and into the tip of the flap, pulling the thread until the beads hang as shown in the photo. Weave in ends.

Following the chart at right, using the tapestry needle and two strands of pearl cotton sew the size 6 beads to the flap as described on page 14, "Adding Beads over Knitted Stitches."

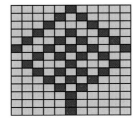

Knitting
■■■▢
Intermediate

Stitching
●●○○
Easy

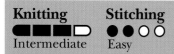

Posy Tote

By using three different colored strands of yarn held together as one, this bag creates an intricate color changing surface with stripes of color that move in and out of the pattern. The flowers and leaves are quick embellishments that easily coordinate since they are yarns used in the bag. You can use any combination of yarn weights to make this bag, making it a great way to use up left over yarn. Look for the original version of this bag featuring a twisted I-cord handle and novelty yarn body in Classic Elite's #9073 Complements pattern booklet.

Finished size
17" (42.5 cm) wide by 15"(37.5) tall with 12" (30 cm) straps

Materials
3 balls (1.75oz/50g, 116yd/106m) sport weight yarn in olive green (2)
2 balls each (1.75oz/50g, 126yd/115m) fingering weight yarn in teal green, smoky gray, forest green, and light green (1)
1 ball (1.75oz/50g, 126yd/115m) fingering weight yarn in white (1)
Size 8 (5 mm) dpn knitting needles at least 8" (20 cm) long
Size 8 (5 mm) 32" (80 cm) cir needles
Size 3 (3.25 mm) knitting needles at least 6" (15 cm) long
Tapestry needle
Stitch markers

This project was made using
3 balls of Dale of Norway's Falk (100% pure new wool, 1.75oz/50g, 116yd/106m) in color #9155 olive green
Dale of Norway's Tiur (60% mohair/40% pure new wool, 1.75oz/50g, 126yd/115m) 2 balls each in colors #7053 teal green, #5371 smoky gray, 7562 forest green, #8533 light green and one ball of #0020 white

Color A: 3 balls olive green
Color B: 2 balls teal green
Color C: 2 balls smoky gray
Color D: 2 balls forest green
Color E: 2 balls light green
Color F: 1 ball white

Gauge in Stockinette Stitch
holding A, B and C tog as one, using the larger needles
15 1/2 sts and 20 rows = 4" (10 cm)

Bag (Worked in the round, beg at center bottom of the bag)

Using dpn and A, B, and C held tog as one, CO 2 sts on ea of three needles – 6 sts total.

Round 1: Knit.

Round 2: Inc 1 in ea st, pm – 12 sts.

Round 3: (Inc 1, k1) rep 6 times – 18 sts.

Round 4: (Inc 1, k2) rep 6 times – 24 sts.

Round 5: (Inc 1, k3) rep 6 times – 30 sts.

Continue with 6 increases in ea round, changing to the circular needles when the knitting is large enough, until you have 22 sts in ea rep – 132 sts.

Work 20 rounds.

Change B to D and work 8 rounds.

Change C to E and work 2 rounds.

Change D to F and work 2 rounds.

Change F to D and work 3 rounds.

Change E to C and work 2 rounds.

Change C and D to E and F and work 2 rounds.

Change E and F to C and D and work 1 round.

Change C and D to E and F and work 4 rounds.

Change E and F to B and C and work 12 rounds, BO.

Straps (Make 2)

Using larger needles and A, B, and C held tog as one, CO 6 sts.

Row 1: K1, p1, k2, p1, k1.

Row 2: K1, p4, k1.

Rows 3 – 70: Rep rows 1 and 2, BO.

Leaves (Make 3)

Using the smaller needles and one strand of pale green yarn, CO 3 sts.

Row 1: Knit.

Row 2 and all even rows: Purl.

Row 3: K1, yo, k1 into back of st, yo, k1 - 5 sts.

Row 5: K2, yo, k1 into back of st, yo, k2 - 7 sts.

Row 7: K3, yo, k1 into back of st, yo, k3 - 9 sts.

Row 9: K4, yo, k1 into back of st, yo, k4 - 11 sts.

Row 11: K5, yo, k1 into back of st, yo, k5 - 13 sts.

Row 13 and 15: Knit.

Row 17: Dec 1, k9, dec 1 - 11 sts.

Row 19: Dec 1, k7, dec 1 - 9 sts.

Row 21: Dec 1, k5, dec 1 - 7 sts.

Row 23: Dec 1, k3, dec 1 - 5 sts.

Row 25: Dec 1, k1, dec 1 - 3 sts.

Row 27: Slip 2 sts as if to knit to the right needle, k1, slip first 2 sts over knitted stitch and off the needle - 1 st remaining.

Weave in ends.

Assembly

Curl the top edge of the bag snuggly onto itself on the right side, stitch in place along the 8th row down from the edge.

Sew the straps to the outside of the bag, centered just below the rolled edge, with the ends spaced about 5" (12.5 cm) apart – see photo for placement. Applique the leaves to the sides of the bag as shown in the photo. Sew the flowers to the bag over the leaves.

Posy (make three)

Using the smaller needles and one strand of white yarn CO 50 sts. Work in St st for 8 rows. Cut the yarn to 12" (30 cm) and pass back through all the sts(1), pulling the tail tight so the knitting gathers into a spiral (2). Tack one end of the knitting to the center front of the spiral(3) and the other end to the back of the spiral(4). Do not block.

1

2

3

4

5 Finished posy

Crazy Quilt Stripes Bag

This easy to knit bag with it's changing stripes can be finished when you are done knitting it, or you can add colorful rows of embroidery, and a lining as well. Crazy quilt stitches are very decorative additions with lots of color changes in the threads you use in your stitching.

Finished size
16" (38 cm) wide by 12" (29 cm) tall, with 18" (43 cm) long straps

Materials
3 balls (90yds/82m) worsted weight muted turquoise yarn (4)
1 ball each (90yds/82m) worsted weight purple, cornflower and maroon colored yarn (4)
Size 7 (4.5 mm) circular needles
Size 6 (4.25 mm) needles
Tapestry needle
Stitch marker
Size 8 pearl cotton in plum and light turquoise
Size 5 pearl cotton in blue, light mulberry and cornflower
Size 12 pearl cotton in variegated purple/blue/pink
If lining bag (optional):
      1 yd of lining fabric
      Sewing machine
      Sewing needle and thread to match lining fabric

This project was made using
Jaeger Matchmaker Merino Aran (100% merino wool, 1.75oz/50g, 90yds/82m) 3 balls of color #754 "Eucalyptus" (turquoise) and one ball each of colors #769 "Prose" (maroon), #629 "Mariner" (cornflower), #775 "Gloxinia" (purple)

Gauge in Stockinette Stitch using larger needles
20 sts and 26 rows = 4" (10 cm)

Bag

Bag bottom:

Using the larger needles and turquoise yarn, CO 30 sts. Knit in St st for 70 rows.

Bag sides:

Continuing from bottom section, beg with right side facing, knit row 71, then working along left side edge of knitting, pick up and k 2 sts for every 3 rows along left side edge of bottom of bag. Pick up and knit ea st along the CO row, then pick up and knit 2 sts for every 3 rows along the rem side, the same as you did for the opposite side, pm – 152 sts.

Knit in the round in St st for 40 rows.

Knit the next rnds in the foll color sequence in St st:

5 rnds in purple
3 rnds in maroon
2 rnds in cornflower
1 rnd in purple
1 rnd in cornflower
2 rnds in maroon
1 rnd in cornflower
4 rnds in purple
5 rnds in cornflower
3 rnds in turquoise

Knit the top border patt as foll:

Rnd 1 and 2: (K1, p1) rep around.
Rnd 3 and 4: (P1, k1) rep around.
Rnd 5 and 6: (K1, p1) rep around.
Rnd 7: Knit.
Rnd 8: Purl.
Rnd 9: Knit.
Turn so wrong side of bag is facing and BO in knit st.
Weave in ends.

Straps (Make two)

Using the smaller needles and turquoise yarn, CO 7 sts, leaving a 10" tail to attach strap to bag.
Row 1 - 150: (K1, p1) rep to last st, k1.
BO, leaving a 10" tail to attach strap to bag.

Assembly

Using the tapestry needle and the tails on the straps, sew the straps to the top edge of the bag, positioning the ends about 2 1/2" (6 cm) from center front and center back.

Embroidery

Stitch the following embroiery stitches over the stripes as indicated below, or experiment with your own designs.

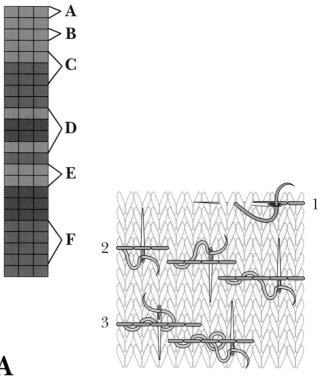

A

Threaded Back Stitch Variation

1 - Using the size 5 pearl cotton in cornflower, stitch back stitches across the row from right to left, making each stitch over one knitted stitch on the front of the bag and passing behind two knitted stitches behind the knitting.

2 - Using the size 5 pearl cotton in blue, pass up and down behind the back stitches as shown above, creating the wave and loop pattern.

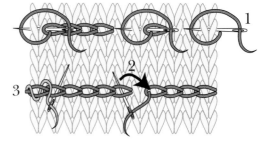

B

Whipped Chain Stitch

1 - Using the size 8 pearl cotton in plum, make chain stitches across the row from left to right, making each stitch over one knitted stitch on the front of the bag.

2 - Join the beginning and ending stitches as shown above.

3 - Using the size 12 pearl cotton, pass up behind the chain stitches as shown above.

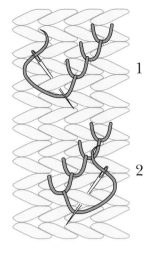

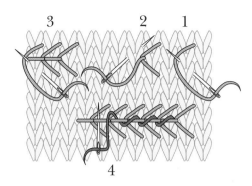

C

Feather Stitch

1 - With the bag facing you with the handles to the left, use the size 5 pearl cotton in cornflower, stitching the loops as shown above, making each stitch slanting to the left one stitch three times.
2 - Continue with the same looped stitches slanting the stitches to the right one stitch three times.
Repeat 1 and 2 creating the zigzag pattern.

E

Fern or Fly Stitch Variation

1 - Using the size 8 pearl cotton in turquoise, *stitch a loop over two rows of stitches, coming up through the knitting one stitch to the left, centered between rows (1). Make a straight stitch over one knitted stitch, coming up one knitted stitch to the right and one row above (2). Repeat from asterisk around the bag (3).
2 - Using the size 5 pearl cotton in cornflower, pass up under the straight stitches (4).

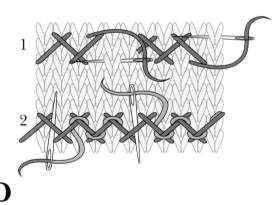

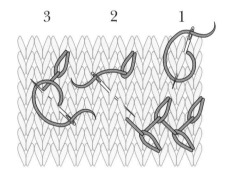

D

Threaded Herringbone Stitch

1 - Using the size 5 pearl cotton in mulberry, stitch as shown, making each stitch over one knitted stitch, working from left to right.
2 - Using the size 8 pearl cotton in turquoise, pass under the center of the herringbone stitches alternately passing up and then down behind the stitch.

F

Feathered Chain Stitch

1 - Using the size 12 pearl cotton, stitch a lazy daisy loop over half of a knitted stitch slanted diagonally down and to the left.
2 - Make a straight stitch diagonally over one knitted stitch in the next row down, coming out of the knitting diagonally down one more row and to the right.
3 - Make another lazy daisy stitch slanted left and upwards, diagonally over one knitted stitch. Repeat step 2 in the opposite direction, then continue the pattern around the bag.

Knitting
■■■□
Intermediate

Stitching
●●○○
Easy

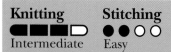

Petite Smocked Bag

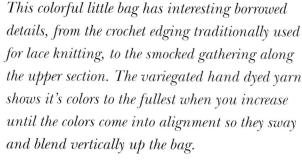

This colorful little bag has interesting borrowed details, from the crochet edging traditionally used for lace knitting, to the smocked gathering along the upper section. The variegated hand dyed yarn shows it's colors to the fullest when you increase until the colors come into alignment so they sway and blend vertically up the bag.

Finished size
Approx. 7" (17.5 cm) tall by 6" (15 cm) wide
at smocking

Materials
1 skein (1.75oz/50g, 175yd/162m) fingering
weight variegated yarn (1)
Size 3 (3.25 mm) double pointed knitting
needles at least 7" (17.5 cm) long
Size E (3.5 mm) crochet hook
Tapestry needle
Stitch markers
Bodkin
48" (120 cm) 1/8" (3 mm) thick decorative
cord

This project was made using the following yarn
One skein of Koigu's Painter's Palette Premium
Merino (KPPPM) (100% merino wool, 1.75oz/
50g, 175yd/162m) color #P623

Gauge in Stockinette Stitch
34 sts and 42 rows = 4" (10 cm)

Notes
Inc = K into front and back of st.
Pm = End of needle counts as marker
(If you want the colors of your yarn to line up vertically as
they do in the sample, you may need to increase more or
less, depending on the yarn you use. If you have more or
less than the 150 sts total, you will have a different number
of stitches at the end of the repeats for the eyelet round
and the crochet edging.)

Bag
CO 6 sts, 2 on each of 3 needles, join into a circle.
Rnd 1: Inc in ea st – 12 sts.
Rnd 2: (Inc, k 1, pm) rep for each pair of sts – 18 sts.
Rnd 3: (Inc, k to marker) rep around – 24 sts.
Rep rnd 3 until there are 25 sts in ea rep – 150 sts total.
Work even for 48 rounds.
To make the eyelet holes for the drawstring, on the next round, (k2tog, yo, k2) rep to last 2 sts, k2.
Knit two more rounds.
Using the crochet hook, (pick up 4 sts off needle, yo, pull through all sts on hk, ch 6) rep around, picking up the rem 6 sts off the needle for the last rep.
Weave in ends.

Smocking
Stitch 2 rows of smocking as shown on the facing page.

Drawstring
Cut the cord in half. Use the bodkin to weave one cord in and out of the eyelets, all the way around the bag. Tie the cord ends together into an overhand knot. Beginning at the opposite end of where the first cord exits the bag, weave the second cord in and out of the eyelets, all the way around the bag. Tie the cord ends together into an overhand knot.

Smocking
Using tapestry needle and 24" (60 cm) length of yarn, stitch smocking pattern, beg 2 rows down from eyelets, working two rows of smocking around bag.

Diamond Smocking Stitch

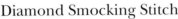

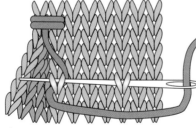

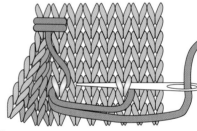

1. Beginning with the yarn coming out on the left side of any stitch 2 rows down from the eyelets, pass the needle from right to left, behind the 4th stitch to the right and the beginning stitch. Keep the thread above the needle and the stitch loose.

2. Take another stitch from right to left, through the fourth stitch to the right again, keeping the thread above the needle. Pull the previous loop tight to gather the fabric, then finish pulling the current stitch in place so it sits below the first stitch.

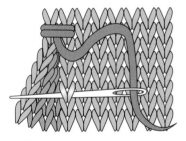

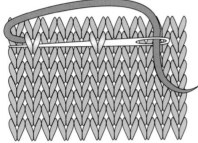

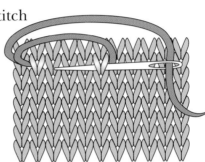

3. Pass the needle from right to left, in the stitch 4 stitches below.

4. Pass the needle from right to left, through the fourth stitch to the right and through the same stitch as in step 3, keeping the thread below the needle. Keep the stitch loose.

5. Take another stitch in the same stitch on the right. Pull the previous loop tight to gather the fabric, then finish pulling the remaining thread through so it sits above the other stitch.

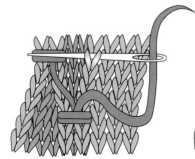

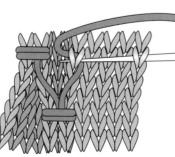

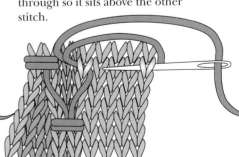

6. Pass the needle from right to left behind the stitch 4 stitches above.

7. Take another stitch from right to left, through the fourth stitch to the right and through the same stitch as in step 6, keeping the thread above the needle. Keep the stitch loose.

8. Take another stitch in the same stitch on the right as in step 2. Repeat steps 3 through 8 around the bag.

59

Section 5
Sweaters

From leaves falling in autumn and snow-flakes drifting into winter, to a day at the beach and fun abstract designs, you'll find a broad range of ideas here for embroidering and embellishing your knitted sweaters. Swiss darning is the main form of embroidery used on these projects, though some also have beading and embroidery stitches that add to the patterns. Most of the synthetic and cotton projects are worked in Stockinette stitch throughout, since the edges don't curl as they do in wool. If you find your knitted edges curling too much, try an inch or so of garter stitch or seed stitch at the bottom of the body and sleeves.

Falling Leaves Sweater

A basic sweater is a great backdrop for bold motifs Swiss darned in rows, or as this sweater was stitched, randomly across the surface. The isolated leaf pattern is one you can use again and again, on bags, hats, or pillows - anywhere you want to add a leaf pattern to your knitting. And the unadorned sweater pattern is a versatile classic.

Sizes
To fit bust sizes
36 (38, 40, 43, 45, 47, 49)"
 /90 (95, 100, 107.5, 112.5, 117.5, 122.5) cm

Knitted Measurements
Bust 38 (40, 42, 45, 47, 49, 51)"
 /95 (100, 105, 112.5, 117.5, 122.5, 127.5) cm
Length 21 1/2 (22, 22 1/2, 22 1/2, 23, 23 1/2, 23 1/2)"
 /54 (55, 56.5, 56.5, 58, 59, 59) cm
Upper Arm 12 1/2 (13, 13 1/2, 14, 14 1/2, 15, 15)"
 /31 (33, 34, 35, 36, 38, 38) cm

Materials
5 (6, 6, 6, 7, 7, 8) skeins (4oz/113g, 190yd/173m) brick red
 worsted weight yarn (4)
Less than1 skein each (4oz/113g, 190yd/173m) worsted
 weight yarn in dark burgundy, light brown
 and dark brown (4)
Size 9 (5.5 mm) at least 14" (35 cm) knitting needles
 and 20" (50 cm) circular knitting needles for neckband
Tapestry needle
Stitch markers
Stitch holders

This project was made using the following yarn
Brown Sheep's Lamb's Pride worsted weight yarn (85% wool/15% mohair, 4oz/113g, 190yd/173m) 6 skeins in color #M-181 "Prairie Fire"(brick red) and one skein each in colors #M-185 "Aubergine"(dark burgundy), #M-175 "Bronze Patina"(light brown) and #M-97 "Rust"(dark brown)

Gauge in Stockinette Stitch
16 sts and 22 rows = 4" (10 cm)

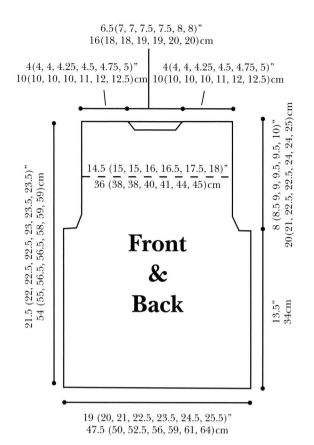

6.5(7, 7, 7.5, 7.5, 8, 8)"
16(18, 18, 19, 19, 20, 20)cm

4(4, 4, 4.25, 4.5, 4.75, 5)"
10(10, 10, 10, 11, 12, 12.5)cm

4(4, 4, 4.25, 4.5, 4.75, 5)"
10(10, 10, 10, 11, 12, 12.5)cm

14.5 (15, 15, 16, 16.5, 17.5, 18)"
36 (38, 38, 40, 41, 44, 45)cm

8 (8.5 9, 9, 9.5, 9.5, 10)"
20(21, 22.5, 22.5, 24, 24, 25)cm

21.5 (22, 22.5, 22.5, 23, 23.5, 23.5)"
54 (55, 56.5, 56.5, 58, 59, 59)cm

Front & Back

13.5"
34cm

19 (20, 21, 22.5, 23.5, 24.5, 25.5)"
47.5 (50, 52.5, 56, 59, 61, 64)cm

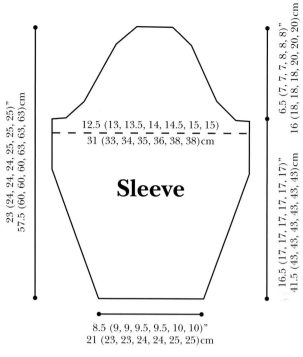

12.5 (13, 13.5, 14, 14.5, 15, 15)
31 (33, 34, 35, 36, 38, 38)cm

Sleeve

6.5 (7, 7, 7, 8, 8, 8)"
16 (18, 18, 18, 20, 20)cm

23 (24, 24, 24, 25, 25, 25)"
57.5 (60, 60, 60, 63, 63, 63)cm

16.5 (17, 17, 17, 17, 17, 17)"
41.5 (43, 43, 43, 43, 43, 43)cm

8.5 (9, 9, 9.5, 9.5, 10, 10)"
21 (23, 23, 24, 24, 25, 25)cm

Back

Using the brick red yarn, CO 76 (80, 84, 90, 94, 98, 102) sts.

Knit in Seed st for 6 rows.

Change to St st, working until piece meas 13 1/2" (34 cm).

Armhole:

BO 3 sts at beg of next 2 rows - 70 (74, 78, 84, 88, 92, 94) sts.

Dec 1 st at ea end on every right side row, 6 (7, 9, 10, 11, 11, 12) times - 58 (60, 60, 64, 66, 70, 72) sts.

Work even in St st until piece meas 20 1/2 (21, 21 1/2, 21 1/2, 22, 22 1/2, 22 1/2)"/ 51 (53, 54, 54, 55, 56, 56)cm.

Neck and Shoulders:

On the next right side row, knit 19 (19, 19, 20 21, 22, 23) sts, move next 20 (22, 22, 24, 24, 26, 26) sts to holder, attach a new ball of yarn and knit 19 (19, 19, 20 21, 22, 23) sts.

Working ea side separately, dec 1 st at neckline on next 3 rows - 16 (16, 16, 17, 18, 19, 20) sts ea shoulder. BO 8 sts at armhole on next row beg at armhole. Work one row. BO rem 8 (8, 8, 9, 10, 11, 12) sts.

Front

Knit the same as the back through armhole dec - 58 (60, 60, 64, 66, 70, 72) sts.

Work even in St st until piece meas 18 (18 1/2, 18 1/2, 18 1/2, 19, 19 1/2, 19 1/2)" / 45 (46, 46, 46, 48, 49, 49)cm.

Neck and Shoulders:

On the next right side row, knit 21 (21, 21, 23, 24, 26, 27) sts, move next 16 (18, 18, 18, 18, 18, 18) sts to holder, attach a new ball of yarn and knit 21 (21, 21, 23, 24, 26, 27) sts.

Knitting ea side separately, dec 1 st at neckline on next 5 (5, 5, 6, 6, 7, 7) rows - 16 (16, 16, 17, 18, 19, 20) sts ea shoulder. Work even in St st until piece meas 1/2" (1 cm) from total length. BO 8 sts at armhole on next row beg at armhole. Work one row. BO rem 8 (8, 8, 9, 10, 11, 12) sts.

Sleeves (make two)

Using the brick red yarn, CO 34 (36, 36, 38, 38, 40, 40) sts.

Knit even in St st for 1" (2 cm).

Cont in St st, inc 1 st ea side every 8th row, 8 (8, 9, 9, 10, 10, 10) times - 50 (52, 54, 56, 58, 60, 60) sts.

Work even in St st until piece meas 16 1/2 (17, 17, 17, 17, 17, 17)" / 41 (43, 43, 43, 43, 43, 43)cm.

Shape cap:

BO 3 sts at beg of next 2 rows - 44 (46, 48, 50, 52, 54, 54) sts.

Dec 1 st at ea end on every right side row, 6 (7, 8, 8, 8, 8, 8) times, then every third row 6 times, then every right side row 3 (3, 3, 3, 4, 4, 4) times.

BO rem 14 (14, 14, 16, 16, 18, 18) sts.

Assembly

Sew front to back at shoulders. Center sleeve at shoulder seam and sew sleeves in place. Sew sleeve seam and front to back at sides.

Neckband

With right side of sweater facing you, pick up and knit 3 sts from right back neck edge, 20 (22, 22, 24, 24, 26, 26) sts from back neck holder, 3 sts from left back neck edge, 16 (16, 18, 18, 18, 19, 19) sts from the left front neck edge, 16 (18, 18, 18, 18, 18, 18) sts from front neck holder, 16 (16, 18, 18, 18, 19, 19) sts from right front neck edge - 74 (78, 82, 84, 84, 88, 88) sts.

Knit in the round in St st for 10 rounds. Reverse direction so the wrong side is facing you and BO loosely in knit stitch.

Embroidery

Using the rem colors of yarn and the tapestry needle stitch the leaf patterns on the sweater, placing them randomly on the sweater as in the sample, or creating a pattern.

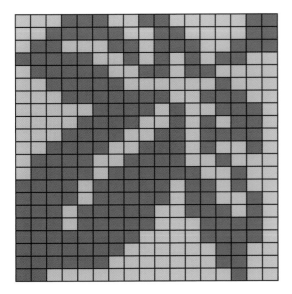

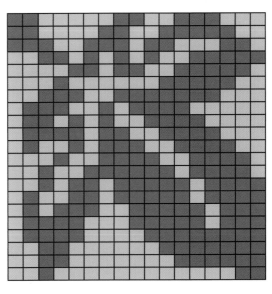

65

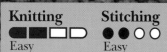
Purple Suede Sweater

This scooped necked sweater combines the textures of suede yarn, with it's subtle color changes, and the sparkly variegated novelty yarn. The simple wavy stripes are easy to stitch in Swiss darning.

Sizes
To fit bust sizes
36 (38, 40, 42, 44, 46, 48)"
    /90 (95, 100, 105, 110, 115, 120) cm

Knitted Measurements
Bust 38 (40, 42, 44, 46, 48, 50)"
    /95 (100, 105, 110, 115, 120, 125) cm
Length 21 (22, 22 1/2, 23, 23 1/2, 24, 25)"
    /52.5 (55, 56, 57.5, 58.5, 60, 62.5) cm
Upper Arm 18 1/2 (19, 20, 20 1/2, 21, 21 1/2, 22)"
    /46 (48, 50, 51, 53, 54, 55) cm

Materials
7 (9, 9,10, 11, 12, 12) balls (120yd/111m) of purple
    worsted weight yarn 🧶4
Less than 1 ball (146yd/135m) of variegated novelty
    worsted weight yarn 🧶4
Size 7 (4.5 mm) at least 14" (35 cm) straight
    knitting needles
Size 6 (4.25 mm) knitting needles at least 14" (35 cm)
    long
Stitch holders
Tapestry needle

This project was made using the following yarn
12 balls of Berroco's Suede (100% nylon, 120yd/111m,
1.75oz/50g) in color #3745 "Calamity Jane"
1 ball of Berroco's Crystal FX (100% nylon, 146yd/
135m, 1.75oz/50g) in color #4803 "Raspberries"

Gauge in Stockinette Stitch
19 sts and 28 rows = 4" (10 cm)

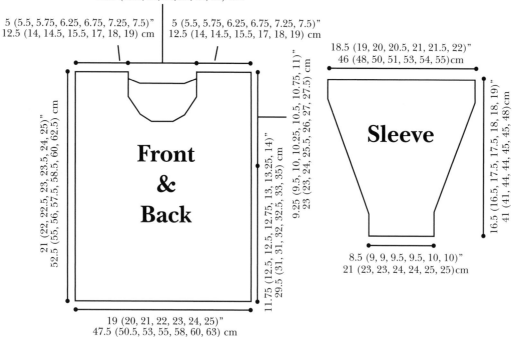

9 (9, 9.5, 9.5, 9.5, 9.5, 10)"
22.5 (22.5, 24, 24, 24, 24, 25) cm

5 (5.5, 5.75, 6.25, 6.75, 7.25, 7.5)"
12.5 (14, 14.5, 15.5, 17, 18, 19) cm

5 (5.5, 5.75, 6.25, 6.75, 7.25, 7.5)"
12.5 (14, 14.5, 15.5, 17, 18, 19) cm

18.5 (19, 20, 20.5, 21, 21.5, 22)"
46 (48, 50, 51, 53, 54, 55)cm

Sleeve

Front & Back

21 (22, 22.5, 23, 23.5, 24, 25)"
52.5 (55, 56, 57.5, 58.5, 60, 62.5) cm

9.25 (9.5, 10, 10.25, 10.5, 10.75, 11)"
23 (23, 24, 25.5, 26, 27, 27.5) cm

11.75 (12.5, 12.5, 12.75, 13, 13.25, 14)"
29.5 (31, 31, 32, 32.5, 33, 35) cm

16.5 (16.5, 17.5, 17.5, 18, 18, 19)"
41 (41, 44, 44, 45, 45, 48)cm

8.5 (9, 9, 9.5, 9.5, 10, 10)"
21 (23, 23, 24, 24, 25, 25)cm

19 (20, 21, 22, 23, 24, 25)"
47.5 (50.5, 53, 55, 58, 60, 63) cm

Back

Using the larger needles and suede yarn, CO 90 (96, 100, 106, 110, 114, 120) sts.
Knit in St st until piece measures 20 (21, 21 1/2, 22, 22 1/2, 23, 24)"/50 (52.5, 53.5, 55, 56, 57.7, 60) cm.

Shape Neck:
On next right side row, k 27 (30, 30, 33, 35, 37, 39) sts, transfer center 36 (36, 38, 40, 40, 40, 42) sts to st holder, attach new ball of yarn and k rem 27 (30, 30, 33, 35, 37, 39) sts.
Work ea side separately.
Dec 1 st ea neck edge every row 3 times - 24 (27, 28, 30, 32, 34, 36) sts ea shoulder.
Knit three more rows even in St st.
BO.

Front

Using the larger needles and purple yarn, CO 90 (96, 100, 106, 110, 114, 120) sts.
Knit in St st until piece measures 14 1/2 (15 1/2, 16, 16, 16 1/2, 16 1/2, 17 1/2)"/36 (39, 40, 40, 41, 41, 44)cm – 108 (108, 112, 112, 115, 115, 122) rows.

Shape Neck:
On next right side row, k 38 (41, 42, 44, 46, 48, 50) sts, transfer center 14 (14, 16, 18, 18, 18, 20) sts to st holder, attach new ball of yarn and k rem 38 (41, 42, 44, 46, 48, 50) sts.
Work ea side separately.
Purl 1 row.
Dec 1 st on neck edge every row 7 times – 31 (34, 35, 37, 39, 41, 43) sts.
Dec 1 st on neck edge every other row 7 times - 24 (27, 28, 30, 32, 34, 36) sts
K even in St st until piece measures the same as the back.
BO.

Sleeves (make two)

Using the larger needles and purple yarn, CO 40 (42, 43, 45, 46, 48, 48) sts.
Knit 8 rows in St st.
Inc 1 st ea end every 4th row 24 (24, 26, 26, 27, 27, 28) times – 88 (90, 95, 97, 100, 102, 104) sts.
Knit 12 more rows even in St st.
BO.

Embroidery

Following the chart at right, embroider the front with the novelty yarn in Swiss darning stitches, continuing the center wave pattern repeat to the bottom edge of the sweater front.

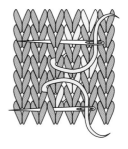

Assembly and Finishing

Block all pieces.
Sew front to back at the shoulders.

Neck Edging:
With the right side of knitting facing you using the smaller needles, pick up and knit 4 sts from the right back neck edge, 36 (36, 38, 40, 40, 40, 42) sts from the back st holder, 4 sts from the left back neck edge, 24 (24, 26, 26, 29, 29, 29) sts from left front neck edge, 14 (14, 16, 18, 18, 18, 20) sts from st holder, and 24 (24, 26, 26, 29, 29, 29) sts from right front neck edge – 106 (106, 114, 118, 124, 124, 128) sts.
Knit two rounds.
Purl one round.
BO loosely in knit stitch.

Sleeves and side seams:
Center the sleeves over the shoulder seams and sew to the sides of the front and back.
Sew the sleeve and front and back side seams together.

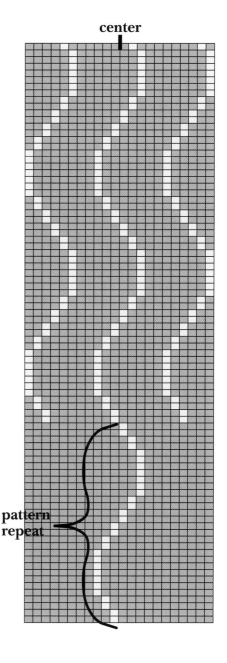

center

pattern
repeat

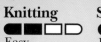

Norwegian Ski Sweater

If you like the Norwegian ski sweater patterns, but don't want to knit the colorwork patterns or work in thin yarn, then this is the pattern for you. The sweater is knit with dropped shoulders and easy shaping with only a few rows of white stripes. Then the Swiss darned pattern is stitched on the front and sleeves before assembly. The soft wool yarn is a joy to work with and the resulting design is a timeless garment you can wear year after year.

Sizes
To fit bust sizes
34 (36, 38, 40, 42, 44, 46)"
    /85 (90, 95, 100, 105, 110, 115) cm

Knitted Measurements
Bust 38 (40, 42, 44, 46, 48, 50)"
    /95 (100, 105, 110, 115, 120, 125) cm
Length 25 (26, 27, 28, 28, 29, 29)"
    /63 (65, 68, 70, 70, 73, 73) cm
Upper Arm 18 (19, 19, 20, 20, 21, 21)"
    /46 (48, 48, 50, 50, 53, 53) cm

Materials
5 (5, 5, 6, 6, 7, 7) 225 yard skeins of worsted weight
    yarn in Blue **4**
1 225 yard skein of worsted weight yarn in White **4**
Size 9 (5.5 mm) at least 14" (35 cm) long knitting
    needles and 20" (50 cm) circular knitting needles
    for neck
Stitch holder
Tapestry needle

This project was made using the following yarn
Lorna's Laces Shepherd Worsted (100% super wash
wool, 225yd/208m) 6 skeins in color #14ns "Denim"
and one skein in color #0ns "Natural"

Gauge in Stockinette Stitch
16 sts and 23 rows = 4" (10 cm)

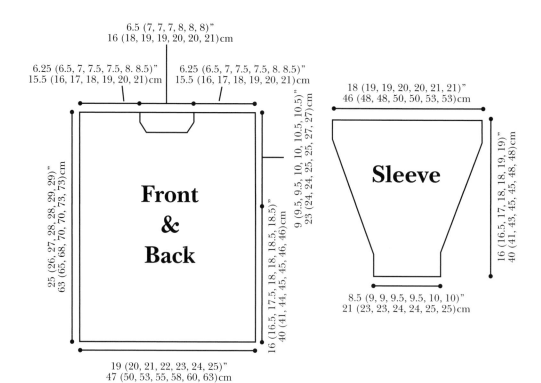

6.5 (7, 7, 7, 8, 8, 8)"
16 (18, 19, 19, 20, 20, 21)cm

6.25 (6.5, 7, 7.5, 7.5, 8. 8.5)"
15.5 (16, 17, 18, 19, 20, 21)cm

6.25 (6.5, 7, 7.5, 7.5, 8. 8.5)"
15.5 (16, 17, 18, 19, 20, 21)cm

Front & Back

25 (26, 27, 28, 28, 29, 29)"
63 (65, 68, 70, 70, 73, 73)cm

9 (9.5, 9.5, 10, 10, 10.5, 10.5)"
23 (24, 24, 25, 25, 27, 27)cm

16 (16.5, 17.5, 18, 18, 18.5, 18.5)"
40 (41, 44, 45, 45, 46, 46)cm

19 (20, 21, 22, 23, 24, 25)"
47 (50, 53, 55, 58, 60, 63)cm

Sleeve

18 (19, 19, 20, 20, 21, 21)"
46 (48, 48, 50, 50, 53, 53)cm

16 (16.5, 17, 18, 18, 19, 19)"
40 (41, 43, 45, 45, 48, 48)cm

8.5 (9, 9, 9.5, 9.5, 10, 10)"
21 (23, 23, 24, 24, 25, 25)cm

Back

Using the blue yarn, CO 76 (80, 84, 88, 92, 96, 100) sts.
Knit in St st until piece meas 24 (25, 26, 27, 27, 28, 28)"/60 (62.5, 65, 67.5, 67.5, 70, 70) cm – 138 (144, 150, 156, 156, 162, 162) rows.

Shape neck:

On next right side row, k 27 (28, 30, 32, 33, 34, 36) sts, transfer center 22 (24, 24, 24, 26, 28, 28) sts to st holder, attach new ball of yarn and k rem 27 (28, 30, 32, 33, 34, 36) sts.

Work ea side separately.

Dec 1 st on neck edge on next two rows – 25 (26, 28, 30, 31, 32, 34) sts.

Work 2 more rows even in St st.

BO.

Front

Using the blue yarn, CO 76 (80, 84, 88, 92, 96, 100) sts.
Work in St st until piece meas 16 (16 1/2, 17 1/2, 18, 18, 18 1/2, 18 1/2)"/40 (41, 44, 45, 45, 46, 46) cm – 91 (93, 99, 103, 103, 106, 106) rows.

Work the foll color patt:

1 row in white
2 rows in blue
1 row in white
19 rows in blue
1 row in white
2 rows in blue
1 row in white
7 (7, 7, 9, 9, 9, 9) rows in blue

Shape neck:

On next right side row, k 32 (33, 35, 37, 39, 40, 41) sts, transfer center 12 (14, 14, 14, 16, 18, 18) sts to st holder, attach new ball of yarn and k rem 32 (33, 35, 37, 39, 40, 41) sts.

Work ea side separately.

Dec 1 st on neck edge on next 7 rows – 25 (26, 28, 30, 31, 32, 34) sts.

Work 10 (14, 14, 14, 14, 17, 17) more rows even in St st.

BO.

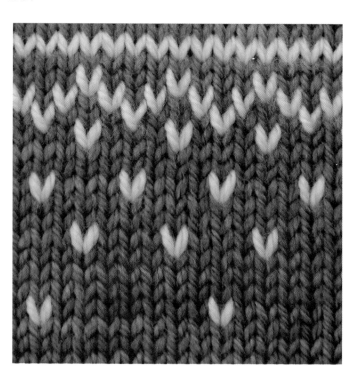

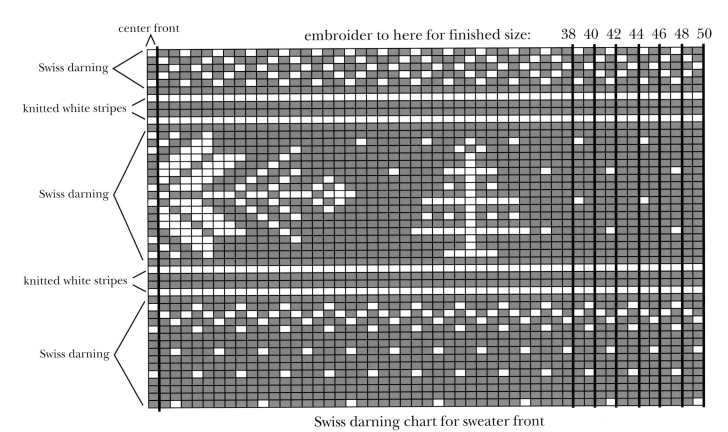

center front

embroider to here for finished size: 38 40 42 44 46 48 50

Swiss darning

knitted white stripes

Swiss darning

knitted white stripes

Swiss darning

Swiss darning chart for sweater front

Sleeves (make two)

Using the blue yarn, CO 34 (36, 36, 38, 38, 40, 40) sts.
Work 2 rows in St st.
Inc 1 st ea end every 4th row 19 (20, 20, 21, 21, 22, 22)
times – 72 (76, 76, 80, 80, 84, 84) sts
and 78 (82, 82, 86, 86, 90, 90) rows.
Work even in the foll color patt:
2 (2, 4, 4, 6, 6) rows in blue
1 row in white
2 rows in blue
1 row in white
8 rows in blue
BO.

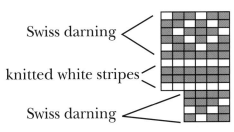

Swiss darning

knitted white stripes

Swiss darning

Swiss darning chart
for sleeves

Embroidery

Following the charts above, embroider the front and sleeves with the white yarn in
swiss darning stitches.

Assembly and Finishing

Sew the front to back at the shoulders.
Collar:
With the right side of knitting facing you, pick up and knit 3 sts from the right back
neck edge, 22 (24, 24, 24, 26, 28, 28) sts from the back st holder, 3 sts from the left
back neck edge, 14 (18, 18, 18, 18, 21, 21) sts from left front neck edge, 12 (14, 14, 14,
16, 18, 18) sts from st holder, and 14 (18, 18, 18, 18, 21, 21) sts from right front neck
edge – 66 (80, 80, 82, 84, 94, 94) sts.
Knit in the round for 3"/7.5cm.
BO loosely.
Sleeves and side seams:
Center the sleeves over the shoulder seams and sew to the sides of the front and back.
Sew the sleeve and front and back side seams tog.

73

Celtic Moss Sweater

Swiss darning easily lends itself to Celtic style designs like this one with it's continually crossing diagonal lines. Stitching the light color first sets your pattern placement, making the remaing large center design color easier to stitch. Stitch the border patterns last. The pattern can also be stitched down the center of the sleeves for added detail.

Sizes
To fit bust sizes
36 (38, 40, 42, 44, 46, 48)"
/90 (95, 100, 105, 110, 115, 120) cm

Knitted Measurements
Bust 38 (40, 42, 44, 46, 48, 50)"
/95 (100, 105, 110, 115, 120, 125) cm
Length 21 (22, 22.5, 23, 23.5, 24, 25)"
/52.5 (55, 56, 58, 59, 60, 62) cm
Upper Arm 18 1/2 (19, 20, 20 1/2, 21, 21 1/2, 22)"
/46 (48, 50, 51, 53, 54, 55) cm

Materials
11 (12, 13, 14, 14, 15, 16) balls (1.75oz/50g, 116yds /106m) of medium green sport weight yarn
Less than 1 ball each (1.75oz/50g, 116yds/106m) of light green and dark green sport weight yarn
Size 6 (4.25 mm) at least 14" (35 cm) long straight knitting needles and 20" (50 cm) circular knitting needles for neck

This project was made using the following yarn
Dale of Norway's Falk (100% pure new wool, 1.75oz/ 50g, 116yds/106m) color #9155 medium green and Tiur (60% mohair/40% pure new wool, 1.75oz/50g, 126yd/115m) one each in colors #8533 light green and #7562, dark green

Gauge in Stockinette Stitch
19 sts and 28 rows = 4" (10 cm)

Front & Back

6.5 (7, 7, 7, 7.5, 8, 8)"
16.5 (17.5, 17.5, 17.5, 18.5, 20, 20)cm

6.25 (6.5, 7, 7.5, 7.75, 8, 8.5)"
15.5 (16.25, 17.5, 18.75, 19.5, 20, 21.25)cm

6.25 (6.5, 7, 7.5, 7.75, 8, 8.5)"
15.5 (16.25, 17.5, 18.75, 19.5, 20, 21.25)cm

Front & Back

21 (22, 22.5, 23, 23.5, 24, 25)"
52.5 (55, 56, 58, 59, 60, 62)cm

9.25 (9.5, 10, 10.25, 10.5, 10.75, 11)"
23 (24, 25, 26, 26, 26, 27)cm

11.75 (12.5, 12.5, 12.75, 13, 13.75, 14)"
29.5 (31, 31, 32, 33, 34, 35)cm

19 (20, 21, 22, 23, 24, 25)"
47.5 (50, 52.5, 55, 57.5, 60, 62.5)cm

Sleeve

18.5 (19, 20, 20.5, 21, 21.5, 22)"
46 (48, 50, 51, 53, 54, 55)cm

Sleeve

16.5 (16.5, 17.5, 17.5, 18, 18, 19)"
46 (48, 50, 51, 53, 54, 55)cm

8.5 (9, 9, 9.5, 9.5, 10, 10)"
21 (23, 23, 24, 24, 25, 25)cm

Notes:
Increase by knitting into the front and back of the stitch.
Decrease by knitting two stitches together as one.

Back
Using the medium green yarn, CO 91 (95, 101, 105, 109, 115, 119) sts.
Work in St st until piece measures 20 (21, 21 1/2, 22, 22 1/2, 23, 24)"/ 50 (52.5, 54, 55, 56, 57.5, 60)cm.

Neck Shaping:
On the next right side row, knit 32 (33, 35, 37, 39, 40, 42) sts, move next 27 (29, 31, 31, 31, 35, 35) sts to holder, attach a new ball of yarn and knit remaining 32 (33, 35, 37, 39, 40, 42) sts.
Working ea side separately, dec 1 st at neckline on next two rows - 30 (31, 33, 35, 37, 38, 40) sts ea side.
Work 4 rows even in St st, BO.

Front
Using the medium green yarn, CO 91 (95, 101, 105, 109, 115, 119) sts.
Work in St st until piece measures 18.5 (18.5, 19, 19, 19, 20, 20)"/ 46 (46, 48, 48, 48, 50, 50)cm.

Neck Shaping:
On the next right side row, knit 38 (39, 41, 43, 45, 46, 48) sts, move next 15 (17, 19, 19, 19, 23, 23) sts to holder, knit remaining 38 (39, 41, 43, 45, 46, 48) sts.
Working ea side separately, dec 1 st at neckline on next 8 rows - 30 (31, 33, 35, 37, 38, 40) sts ea side.
Work 18 (18, 20, 20, 20, 20, 20) rows even in St st, BO.

Sleeves (make two)
Using the medium green yarn, CO 40 (42, 43, 45, 46, 48, 48) sts.
Work even in St st for 12 rows.
Continuing in St st, inc 1 st ea side every 4th row, 24 (24, 26, 26, 27, 27, 28) times - 88 (90, 95, 97, 100, 102, 104) sts.
Work even in St st for 8 rows, BO.

Assembly

Sew front to back at shoulders. Center sleeve at shoulder seam and sew sleeves in place. Sew sleeve seam and front to back at sides.

Neckband

With right side of sweater facing you, using the circular needles, pick up and knit 4 sts from right back neck edge, 27 (29, 31, 31, 31, 35, 35) sts from back neck holder, 4 sts from left back neck edge, 16 (16, 18, 18, 18, 18, 18) sts from the left front neck edge, 15 (17, 19, 19, 19, 23, 23) sts from front neck holder, 16 (16, 18, 18, 18, 18, 18) sts from right front neck edge - 82 (86, 94, 94, 94, 102, 102) sts.
Knit in the round in St st for 15 rounds. Reverse direction so wrong side of knitting is facing you and BO loosely in knit st.

Embroidery

Using the dark and light green yarn and the tapestry needle stitch the pattern repeats shown below in Swiss darning stitch on the center front of the sweater, beginning about 2" (5 cm) down from the top neck edge and continuing the pattern repeat to about 2" (5 cm) from the bottom edge of the sweater.

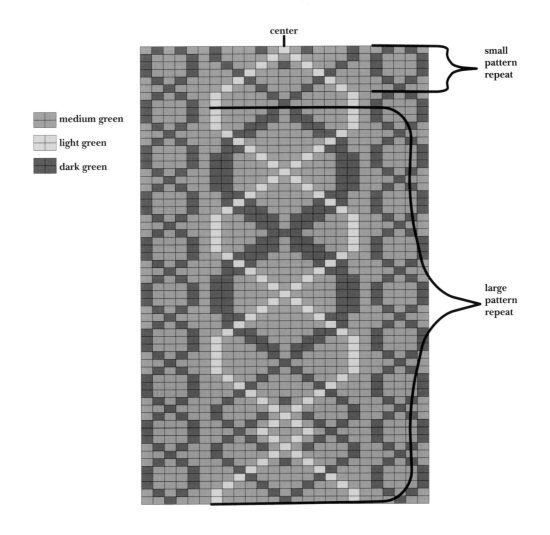

center

small pattern repeat

medium green
light green
dark green

large pattern repeat

Cowlneck Sweater

Sometimes a simple design just needs a little touch of something extra to make it special. With subtle color and a flattering cowl neckline, this sweater is finished off with a little swirl on the sleeves in chain stitch, creating an understated elegance that needs no other embellishment.

Sizes
To fit bust sizes
34 (36, 38, 40, 42, 44, 46)"
    /85 (90, 95, 100, 105, 110, 115) cm

Knitted Measurements
Bust 36 (38, 40, 42, 44, 46, 48)"
    /90 (95, 100, 105, 110, 115, 120) cm
Length 21 1/2 (22, 22 1/2, 23, 23 1/2, 24, 24 1/2)"
    /54 (55, 56, 57.5, 59, 60, 61) cm
Upper Arm 12 1/2 (13, 13 1/2, 14, 14 1/2, 15, 15)"
    /31 (32.5, 34, 35, 36, 37.5, 37.5) cm

Materials
7 (7, 8, 8, 9, 9, 10) skeins (3.5oz/100g, 163yd/150m)
    pale silver/turquoise worsted weight yarn 4
Size 7 (4.5 mm) at least 14" (35 cm) straight knitting
    needles and size 24" (60 cm) circular knitting
    needles for collar
Size 8 teal pearl cotton or embroidery thread
Chenille or embroidery needle
Tapestry needle

This project was made using the following yarn and thread
Patons' Katrina (92% rayon/8% polyester, 3.5oz/100g, 163yd/150m) color #10205 "Glacier"

Caron's Impressions (50% silk/50% wool, 36yd/33m) color #7022

Gauge in Stockinette Stitch
20 sts and 34 rows = 4" (10 cm)

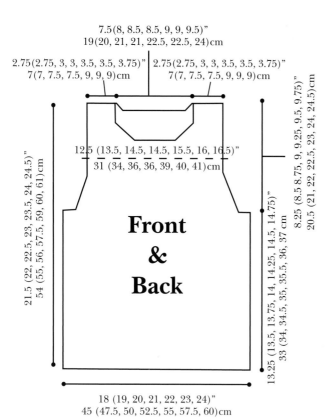

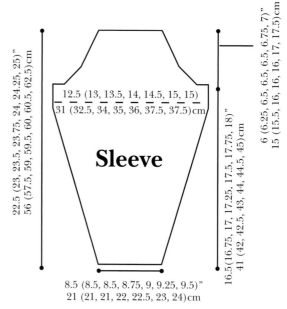

Back

Using the straight needles CO 90 (95, 100, 105, 110, 115, 120) sts.

Work in St st until piece measures 13 1/4 (13 1/2, 13 3/4, 14, 14 1/4, 14 1/2, 14 3/4)" / 33 (33.5, 34, 35, 35.5, 36, 37) cm.

Armhole Shaping:

BO 3 (4, 4, 5, 5, 6, 6) sts at beg of next 2 rows - 84 (87, 92, 95, 100, 103, 108) sts.

Dec 1 st at ea end on every right side row, 10 (10, 10, 11, 11, 12, 12) times - 64 (67, 72, 73, 78, 79, 84) sts.

Work even in St st until piece measures 21 (21 1/2, 22, 22 1/2, 23, 23 1/2, 24)"/ 52.5 (54, 55, 56, 57.5, 58.5, 60)cm.

Neck and Shoulders:

On next right side row, k 16 (17, 18, 18, 20, 20, 21) sts, attach a new ball of yarn and BO center 32 (33, 36, 37, 38, 39, 42) sts, k rem 16 (17, 18, 18, 20, 20, 21) sts.

Working ea side separately, dec 1 st at neck edge every row 3 times, - 13 (14, 15, 15, 17, 17, 18) sts.
At the same time:
BO 5 sts at the beg of the next armhole edge, twice.
BO remaining sts.

Front

Knit the same as the back through armhole dec - 64 (67, 72, 73, 78, 79, 84) sts.

Work even in St st until piece meas 16 1/2 (16 3/4, 17, 17 1/2, 18, 18 1/4, 18 1/2)" / 41 (42, 42.5, 44, 45, 45.5, 46)cm.

Neck and Shoulders:

On next right side row, k 27 (28, 29, 29, 31, 31, 32) sts, attach a new ball of yarn and BO center 10 (11, 14, 15, 16, 17, 20) sts, k rem 27 (28, 29, 29, 31, 31, 32) sts.

Knitting ea side separately, dec 1 st at neckline on next 7 rows, then every other row 7 times - 13 (14, 15, 15, 17, 17, 18) sts. Work even in St st until piece meas 1/2" (1 cm) from total length. BO 5 sts at beg of next armhole edge twice. BO remaining sts.

Sleeves (make two)

CO 42 (42, 43, 44, 46, 47, 48) sts.

Knit even in St st for 2 rows.

Cont in St st, inc 1 st ea side every 10th row, 10 (12, 12, 13, 13, 14, 14) times - 62 (66, 67, 70, 72, 75, 76) sts.

Work even in St st until piece meas 16 1/2 (16 3/4, 17, 17 1/4, 17 1/2, 17 3/4, 18)"/ 41 (42, 42.5, 43, 43.5, 44, 45)cm.

Shape cap:

BO 3 (4, 4, 5, 5, 6, 6) sts at beg of next 2 rows - 56 (58, 59, 60, 62, 63, 64) sts.

Dec 1 st at ea end on every right side row twice, then every third row 15 (16, 16, 16, 17, 17, 17) times, then every right side row twice.

BO rem 18 (18, 19, 20, 20, 21, 22) sts.

Assembly

Sew front to back at shoulders. Center sleeve at shoulder seam and sew sleeves in place. Sew sleeve seam and front to back at sides.

Cowlneck Collar

With right side of sweater facing you and using the circular needles, pick up and knit 36 (37, 40, 41, 42, 43, 46) sts from back neck edge, 24 (25, 27, 27, 27, 28, 29) sts from the left front neck edge, 10 (11, 14, 15, 16, 17, 20) sts from center front neck BO edge, 24 (25, 27, 27, 27, 28, 29) sts from right front neck edge - 94 (98, 108, 110, 112, 116, 124) sts.
Knit in the round in St st for 94 rounds. BO loosely.
Fold the collar to inside and sew to neckline edge.
Fold in half again towards right side so collar drapes as shown in photo.

Embroidery

To transfer the design onto the bottom of each sleeve, first trace the image onto a piece of paper, then cut out on the dotted lines. Using a contrasting thread, stitch the pattern in small straight stitches, centered at the bottom of the sleeve, about 1/2" (1 cm) from the edge. Remove the paper. Now, using the the embroidery thread and needle, chain stitch the design, removing your straight stitches as you stitch.

Pretty in Pink Cotton Tank

Embroider this feminine warm weather tank with Swiss darning in a darker shade of pink cotton blend yarn. If you begin the pattern at the center top of the design, you will ensure your image is centered on the tank. Instructions include the option of the crochet armhole edging shown, or a knitted armhole edging the same as the neckline.

Sizes
To fit bust sizes
34 (36, 38, 40, 42, 44, 46)"
  /85 (90, 95, 100, 105, 110, 115) cm

Knitted Measurements
Bust 36 (38, 40, 42, 44, 47, 49)"
  /90 (95, 100, 105, 110, 117.5, 122.5) cm
Length 20 (21, 21 1/2, 22, 22 1/2, 23, 23 1/2)"
  /50 (52, 54, 55, 56, 57, 59) cm

Materials
3 (3, 3, 3, 4, 4) skeins (3.5oz/100g, 192yd/177m)
  light pink worsted weight yarn (4)
Less than 1 skein (3.5oz/100g, 192yd/177m) dark pink
  worsted weight yarn (4)
Size 8 (5 mm) 16" (40 cm) and 32" (80 cm) circular
  knitting needles
Tapestry needle
Stitch holder
For crochet armhole edging version: size H crochet hook

This project was made using the following yarn
Cascade's Sierra (80% pima cotton/20% wool, 3.5oz/
100g, 192yd/177m) 3 skeins in color #15 light pink and
one skein in color # 17 fuschia

Gauge in Stockinette Stitch
18 sts and 24 rows = 4" (10 cm)

Notes
Inc = Knit into front and back of stitch
Dec = Knit two together as one
Seams were worked in mattress stitch.

Back

Using the light pink yarn, CO 72 (74, 78, 83, 87, 94, 99) sts.

Knit 1 row. Purl 1 row.

Knit the next row decreasing 1 st ea side - 70 (72, 76, 81, 85, 92, 97) sts.

Purl 1 row.

Work 18 rows in St st.

Knit the next row decreasing 1 st ea side - 68 (70, 74, 79, 83, 90, 95) sts.

Purl 1 row. Knit 1 row. Purl 1 row.

Continue in St st, increasing 1 st ea side on the next row and then every 6th row 6 (7, 7, 7, 7, 7, 7) times - 82 (86, 90, 95, 99, 106, 111) sts.

Purl 1 row.

Continue in St st until piece meas 11 1/2 (12 1/2, 12 1/2, 12 1/2, 12 1/2, 12 1/2, 12 1/2)" / 29 (31, 31, 31, 31, 31, 31) cm.

Armhole Shaping:
BO 4 (5, 5, 5, 5, 6, 7) sts at the beg of the next 2 rows - 74 (76, 80, 85, 89, 94, 97) sts.

Dec 1 st ea side every right side row 8 (8, 8, 10, 11, 13, 13) times - 58 (60, 64, 65, 67, 68, 71) sts.

Neck and shoulder shaping:
On next right side row, k 23 (23, 25, 25, 26, 26, 26) sts, transfer center 12 (14, 14, 15, 15, 16, 19) sts to holder, attach new ball of yarn and knit rem 23 (23, 25, 25, 26, 26, 26) sts.

Working ea side separately, dec 1 st at neck edge every row 6 times, then every other row 6 times - 11 (11, 13, 13, 14, 14, 14) sts.

Purl 1 row.

Work even in St st for 14 (14, 18, 18, 18, 18, 20) rows.

BO 7 sts at the beg of the next armhole edge.

BO remaining sts at the beg of the next armhole edge.

Front

Work the same as the back.

Assembly

Sew front to back at shoulders and side seams.

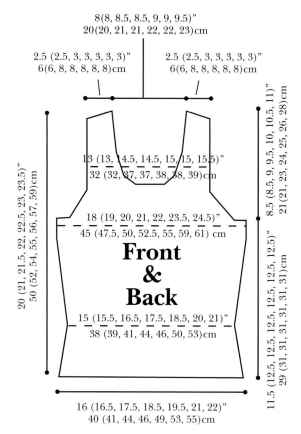

Neck Edging

With right side of sweater facing you, using the circular needles and light pink yarn, pick up and knit 22 (22, 24, 24, 24, 24, 26) sts from right back neck edge, 12 (14, 14, 15, 15, 16, 19) sts from back neck holder, 22 (22, 24, 24, 24, 24, 26) sts from left back neck edge, 22 (22, 24, 24, 24, 24, 26) sts from the left front neck edge, 12 (14, 14, 15, 15, 16, 19) sts from front neck holder, 22 (22, 24, 24, 24, 24, 26) sts from right front neck edge - 112 (116, 124, 126, 126, 128, 142) sts.

Knit 1 round.

Purl 1 round.

Reverse direction and BO loosely.

Armhole Edging - Crochet version

With right side of sweater facing you and the light colored pink yarn, single crochet around the armhole, beginning at the side seam. Weave in ends.

Repeat for the other armhole.

Armhole Edging - Knitted version

With right side of sweater facing you, using the 16" (40 cm) needles and light pink yarn, pick up and knit 34 (34, 36, 38, 41, 43, 45) sts from the back armhole edge and 34 (34, 36, 38, 41, 43, 45) sts from the front armhole edge - 68 (68, 72, 76, 82, 86, 90) sts.

Knit 1 round.

Purl 1 round.

Reverse direction and BO loosely.

Embroidery

Using the dark pink yarn and the tapestry needle stitch the pattern below, centered on the front of the top, beginning the upper most stitches 9 (10, 10, 11, 12, 12) rows below the beginning of the neck edging.

center

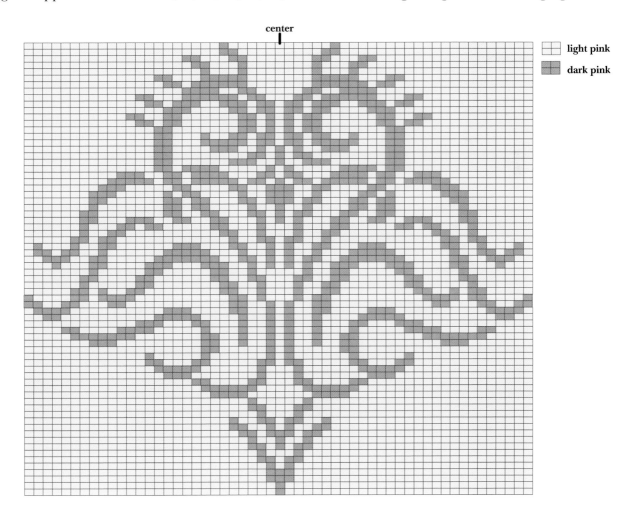

light pink

dark pink

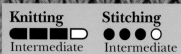

Knitting
■■■▫
Intermediate

Stitching
●●●○
Intermediate

Ocean Waves Cotton Tank

This top is perfect for a day at the beach with it's own soft sandy beach, white foam surf, cool ocean waves, and blue sky. Made the same as the Pretty in Pink Tank on page 82, but in a larger gauge yarn, these easy stripes are made into ocean waves with just a touch of Swiss darning. Make it with it's subtle ocean theme, or add to the design by finding ocean themed buttons and appliques to sew along the beach, ocean and sky.

Sizes
To fit bust sizes
34 (36, 38, 40, 42, 44, 46)"
  /85 (90, 95, 100, 105, 110, 115) cm

Knitted Measurements
Bust 36 (38, 40, 42, 44, 47, 49)"
  /90 (95, 100, 105, 110, 117.5, 122.5) cm
Length 19 (20, 20 1/2, 21, 21 1/2, 22, 22 1/2)"
  /47.5 (50, 51, 52.5, 54, 55, 56) cm

Materials
2 skeins (3.5oz/100g, 140yd/151m) light blue worsted weight yarn 🧶**4**
1 skein each (3.5oz/100g, 140yd/151m) worsted weight yarn in medium blue, mint green, gray/green, light tan, medium tan and variegated light blue 🧶**4**
Size 8 (5 mm) 16" (40 cm) and 32" (80 cm)
  circular knitting needles
Tapestry needle

This project was made using the following yarn
Plymouth Yarn's Fantasy Natural (100% mercerized cotton, 3.5oz/100g, 140yd/151m) 2 skeins in color #8012 light blue, and one skein each in colors # 2574 medium blue, #5424 mint green, #8013 gray/green, #7650 light tan, #7360 medium tan, and #9415 variegated light blue

Gauge in Stockinette Stitch
16 sts and 22 rows = 4" (10 cm)

Back

Work in St st throughout.

Using the light tan yarn and larger needles, CO 64 (66, 70, 74, 78, 84, 88) sts.

Work 2 rows.

Knit the next row decreasing 1 st ea side - 62 (64, 68, 72, 76, 82, 86) sts.

Work 5 more rows.

Work 6 rows in medium tan yarn.

Work 3 rows in variegated blue.

Change to medium blue yarn and purl 1 row.

Knit the next row decreasing 1 st ea side - 60 (62, 66, 70, 74, 80, 84) sts.

Purl 1 row. Knit 1 row. Purl 1 row.

Change to gray/green yarn.

Continue in St st, increasing 1 st ea side every 5th row 6 (7, 7, 7, 7, 7, 7) times - 72 (76, 80, 84, 88, 94, 98) sts.

Purl 1 row.

Continue in St st until piece meas 11 (12, 12, 12, 12, 12, 12)" / 27.5 (30, 30, 30, 30, 30, 30) cm, at the same time working the foll color sequence:

8 rows gray/green

14 rows light blue

8 rows mint green

6 rows gray/green

4 rows light blue

4 rows medium blue

Change to light blue yarn for remainder of knitting.

Armhole Shaping:

BO 5 (6, 6, 7, 8, 9, 9) sts at the beg of the next 2 rows - 62 (64, 68, 70, 72, 76, 80) sts.

Dec 1 st ea side every right side row 7 (7, 8, 9, 9, 10, 11) times - 48 (50, 52, 52, 54, 56, 58) sts.

Work even until piece meas 15 (15 1/2, 15 1/2, 16, 16, 16, 16 1/2)" / 37.5 (39, 39, 40, 40, 40, 41) cm.

Neck and shoulder shaping:

On next right side row, k 19 (19, 20, 20, 21, 22, 22) sts, transfer center 10 (12, 12, 12, 12, 12, 14) sts to holder, attach new ball of yarn and knit rem 19 (19, 20, 20, 21, 22, 22) sts.

Working ea side separately, dec 1 st at neck edge every row 6 times, then every other row 5 times - 8 (8, 9, 9, 10, 11, 11) sts.

Purl 1 row.

Work even in St st until piece meas total length less 1/2" (1 cm).

BO 5 sts at the beg of the next armhole edge on ea side. BO remaining sts at the beg of the next armhole edge on ea side.

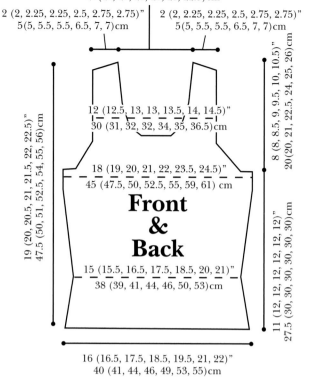

8(8.5, 8.5, 8.5, 8.5, 8.5, 9)"
20(21, 21, 21, 21, 21, 22.5)cm

2 (2, 2.25, 2.25, 2.5, 2.75, 2.75)"
5(5, 5.5, 5.5, 6.5, 7, 7)cm

2 (2, 2.25, 2.25, 2.5, 2.75, 2.75)"
5(5, 5.5, 5.5, 6.5, 7, 7)cm

8 (8, 8.5, 9, 9.5, 10, 10.5)"
20(20, 21, 22.5, 24, 25, 26)cm

12 (12.5, 13, 13, 13.5, 14, 14.5)"
30 (31, 32, 32, 34, 35, 36.5)cm

19 (20, 20.5, 21, 21.5, 22, 22.5)"
47.5 (50, 51, 52.5, 54, 55, 56)cm

18 (19, 20, 21, 22, 23.5, 24.5)"
45 (47.5, 50, 52.5, 55, 59, 61) cm

Front & Back

15 (15.5, 16.5, 17.5, 18.5, 20, 21)"
38 (39, 41, 44, 46, 50, 53)cm

8 (8, 8.5, 9, 9.5, 10, 10.5)"
20(20, 21, 22.5, 24, 25, 26)cm

11 (12, 12, 12, 12, 12, 12)"
27.5 (30, 30, 30, 30, 30, 30)cm

16 (16.5, 17.5, 18.5, 19.5, 21, 22)"
40 (41, 44, 46, 49, 53, 55)cm

Front

Work the same as the back.

Assembly

Sew front to back at shoulders and side seams.

Neck Edging

With right side of sweater facing you, using the longer needles and light blue yarn, pick up and knit 16 (18, 20, 20, 22, 22, 24) sts from right back neck edge, 10 (12, 12, 12, 12, 12, 14) sts from back neck holder, 16 (18, 20, 20, 22, 22, 24) sts from left back neck edge, 16 (18, 20, 20, 22, 22, 24) sts from the left front neck edge, 10 (12, 12, 12, 12, 12, 14) sts from front neck holder, 16 (18, 20, 20, 22, 22, 24) sts from right front neck edge - 88 (100, 108, 108, 116, 116, 128) sts.

Knit 1 round. Purl 1 round.

Turn so wrong side is facing and BO loosely in St st.

Armhole Edging

With right side of sweater facing you, using the shorter needles and light blue yarn, pick up and knit 36 (36, 39, 39, 43, 44, 46) sts from the back armhole edge and 36 (36, 39, 39, 43, 44, 46) sts from the front armhole edge - 72 (72, 78, 78, 86, 88, 92) sts.

Knit 1 round.

Purl 1 round.

Turn so wrong side is facing and BO loosely in St st.

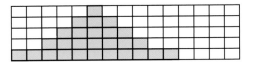

Embroidery

Using the tapestry needle and the same colored yarn as the row below, stitch the wave patterns in Swiss darning on the front of the top, in medium blue, gray/green and light blue, making four waves above the stripe of the same color, spacing the waves 4 stitches apart and offsetting the waves as shown in the photo.

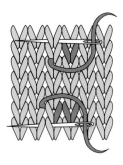

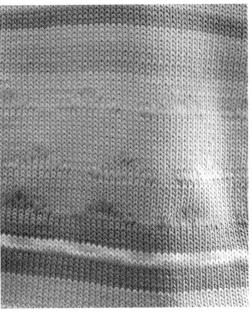

Knitting
◼◼◼◻
Intermediate

Stitching
●●●○
Intermediate

Men's Vest

Combining knitted stripes with Swiss darning and various embroidery stitches adds color and detail to a basic men's vest. You can work the gray zigzag color pattern and the the blue and brown check pattern in Swiss darning, or you can knit them in two stranded colorwork knitting. Either way, they look the same.

Sizes
To fit chest sizes
36 (38, 40, 42, 44, 46, 48)"
    /90 (95, 100, 105, 110, 115, 120) cm

Knitted Measurements
Chest 38 (40, 42, 44, 46, 48, 50)"
    /95 (100, 105, 110, 115, 120, 125) cm
Length 21 (22, 22, 23, 24, 25, 26)"
    /52.5 (55, 55, 57.5, 60, 62.5, 65) cm

Materials
3 (3, 4, 4, 4, 5) skeins (1.75oz/50g, 109yds/101m) sport weight yarn in brown ②
2 skeins each (1.75oz/50g, 109yds/101m) sport weight yarn in plum and medium green ②
One skein each (1.75oz/50g, 109yds/101m) sport weight yarn in wheat, blue, and gray ②
Size 6 (4 mm) 24" and 32" circular knitting needles
Split ring marker
Tapestry needle

This project was made using the following yarn
Classic Elite's Inca Alpaca (100% alpaca, 1.75oz/50g, 109yds/101m) 4 skeins in color #1168 "Cowhide Helmet Brown" (brown), 2 skeins in #1142 "Cajamaica Maroon" (plum), 2 skeins in #1135 "Cala Cala Moss" (medium green), and one skein each in #1117 "Gold Finch" (wheat), #1146 "Island of the Sun" (blue), and #1176 "Gaucho Grey Heather" (gray)

Gauge in Stockinette Stitch
19 sts and 24 rows = 4" (10 cm)

Back

Using medium green yarn, CO 90 (95, 100, 105, 109, 114, 119) sts. Knit in St st for 9 rows. Mark row with split ring marker. Bottom of vest will be folded up at this point.

Cont in St st in the following stripe pattern, until piece measures 11(11 1/2, 11 1/2, 12, 12 1/2, 13, 13)" 27.5 (29, 29, 30, 31, 32.5, 32.5) cm from the marked row:

9 more rows of medium green
   (18 total from beginning)
1 row blue
2 rows wheat
22 rows plum
1 row blue
2 rows wheat
6 rows blue
2 rows wheat
1 row blue
Remaining rows in brown, to length noted above.

Armhole:
BO 5 (6, 7, 8, 9, 10, 11) sts at beg of next 2 rows - 80 (83, 86, 89, 91, 94, 97) sts.
Dec 1 st at ea end on every right side row 8 times - 64 (67, 70, 73, 75, 78, 81) sts.
Work even in St st until piece meas 20 (21, 21, 22, 23, 24, 25)"/ 50 (52.5, 52.5, 55, 57.5, 60, 62.5)cm.

Neck and Shoulders:
On next right side row, k 20 (21, 21, 22, 22, 23, 23) sts, transfer center 24 (25, 28, 29, 31, 32, 35) sts to st holder, attach new ball of yarn and k rem 20 (21, 21, 22, 22, 23, 23) sts.
Work ea side separately.
Purl 1 row.
Dec 1 st ea neck edge every right side row 3 times - 17 (18, 18, 19, 19, 20, 20) sts ea shoulder.
On the next three rows, BO 6 sts on the armhole edge, twice. BO rem stitches.

Left Front

Using medium green yarn, CO 43 (45, 48, 50, 52, 55, 57) sts.
Work the same as the back to just before armhole.

Armhole:
BO 5 (6, 7, 8, 9, 10, 11) sts at beg of next right side row - 38 (39, 41, 42, 43, 45, 46) sts.
Dec 1 st at the beg of every right side row 8 times - 30 (31, 33, 34, 35, 37, 38) sts.

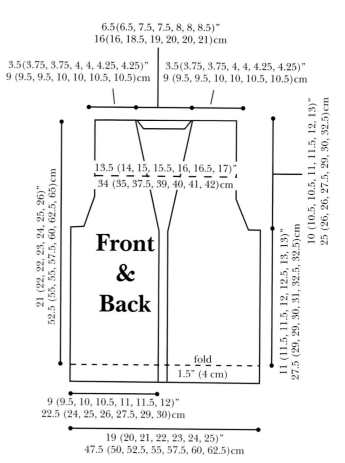

6.5(6.5, 7.5, 7.5, 8, 8, 8.5)"
16(16, 18.5, 19, 20, 20, 21)cm

3.5(3.75, 3.75, 4, 4, 4.25, 4.25)"
9 (9.5, 9.5, 10, 10, 10.5, 10.5)cm

3.5(3.75, 3.75, 4, 4, 4.25, 4.25)"
9 (9.5, 9.5, 10, 10, 10.5, 10.5)cm

13.5 (14, 15, 15.5, 16, 16.5, 17)"
34 (35, 37.5, 39, 40, 41, 42)cm

Front & Back

21 (22, 22, 23, 24, 25, 26)"
52.5 (55, 55, 57.5, 60, 62.5, 65)cm

10 (10.5, 10.5, 11, 11.5, 12, 13)"
25 (26, 26, 27.5, 29, 30, 32.5)cm

11 (11.5, 11.5, 12, 12, 12.5, 13, 13)"
27.5 (29, 29, 30, 31, 32.5, 32.5)cm

fold
1.5" (4 cm)

9 (9.5, 10, 10.5, 11, 11.5, 12)"
22.5 (24, 25, 26, 27.5, 29, 30)cm

19 (20, 21, 22, 23, 24, 25)"
47.5 (50, 52.5, 55, 57.5, 60, 62.5)cm

At the same time as armhole decreases, dec 1 st on the center front side every 4th row 13 (13, 15, 15, 16, 17, 17) times - 17 (18, 18, 19, 19, 20, 21) sts after all dec.
Work even in St st until piece meas 20 1/2 (21 1/2, 21 1/2, 22 1/2, 23 1/2, 24 1/2, 25 1/2)"/ 51 (54, 54, 56, 59, 61, 64)cm. BO 6 sts at the armhole edge of the next 2 right side rows. BO rem sts.

Right Front

Repeat all instructions for Left Front, reversing dec.

Assembly

Block all pieces. Sew front to back at shoulders and sides.
Turn bottom edge of vest to wrong side so 10 rows of the green knitting are on the front of the vest, and sew in place to inside of knitting. Steam block folded edge.

Neckband

Using the longer cir needles, with right side facing you, beg at the lower corner of right front, pick up and knit 3 sts for every 4 rows along center front, 2 sts at beg of center front dec, 1 st for every row along dec of center front, 3 sts for every 4 rows or sts along rem sts of center front and all sts on back to center back. Repeat pick up sequence for other half of vest back and center front edge. Work 3 rows in garter st. BO.

Armhole Ribbing

Using the shorter cir needles, with right side facing you, pick up and knit 68 (70, 70, 76, 80, 84, 92) sts from right front armhole and 68 (70, 70, 76, 80, 84, 92) sts from right back armhole - 136 (140, 140, 152, 160, 168, 184) sts total. Knit in k2, p2 rib for 6 rows. BO in patt.

Embroidery

Using the tapestry needle embroider the stripes as follows:
1 - Swiss darning, brown on the 6-row blue stripe, gray on the 22 row plum stripe.
2 - Half cross stitch in green on the yellow stripes as shown below.
3 - Herringbone stitch in blue over 3 rows of plum as shown below.
4 - Buttonhole stitch in blue over 2 rows at the fold of the green yarn.

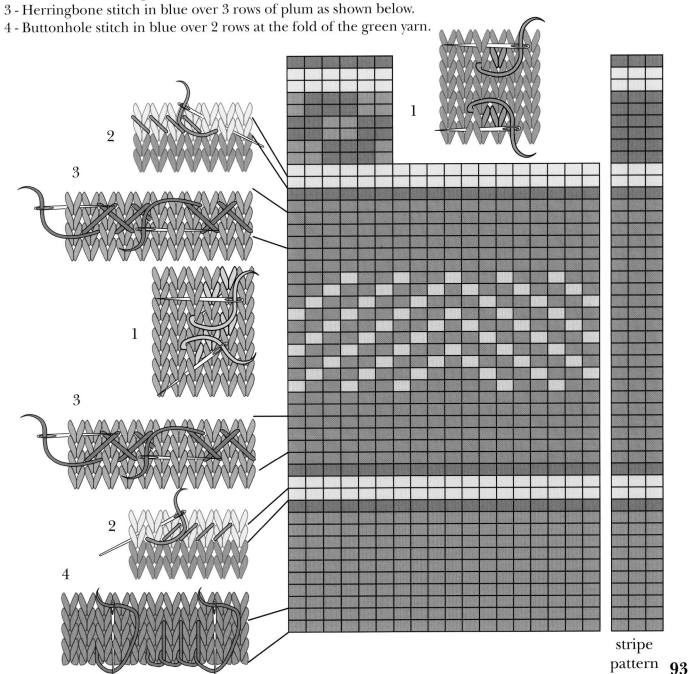

stripe
pattern **93**

Tunic Sweater Jacket

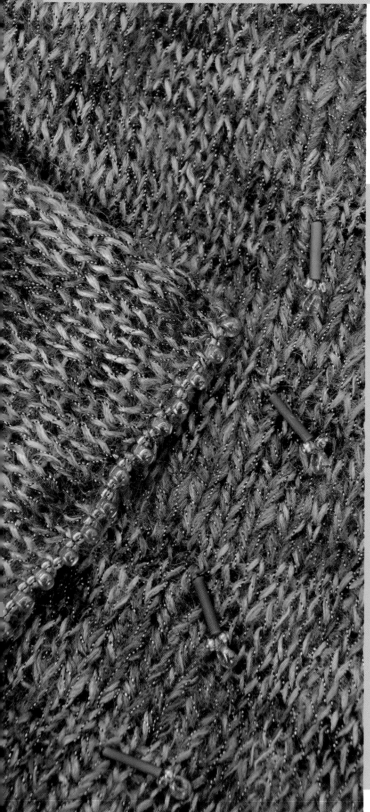

Knitting with thin yarn makes this buttonless jacket lightweight and equally at home over a skirt and blouse or a pair of jeans. You can stitch the Swiss darned triangles down just one side of the jacket as shown, or on both sides and the center back as well. The beads along the neck and sleeves help strengthen and define edges, and the little dangles on the triangles create movement. Your final touch is to find, or make, a special pin for the neckline.

Sizes
To fit bust sizes
36 (38, 40, 42, 44, 46, 48)"
  /90 (95, 100, 105, 110, 115, 120) cm

Knitted Measurements
Bust 40 (42, 44, 46, 48, 50, 52)"
  /100 (105, 110, 115, 120, 125, 130) cm
Length 30 (31, 32, 33, 34, 35, 36)"
  /75 (77.5, 80, 82.5, 85, 87.5, 90) cm
Upper Arm 19 (19 1/2, 20, 20 1/2, 20 1/2, 21, 21 1/2)"
  /47.5 (49, 50, 51, 51, 52.5, 54) cm

Materials
6 (6, 6, 7, 7, 8, 9) balls (1.75oz/50g, 198yd/180m)
  variegated green fingering weight yarn 〈❶〉
Less than 1 ball (1.75oz/50g, 198yd/180m)
  variegated blue fingering weight yarn 〈❶〉
Size 8 (5 mm) at least 14" (35 cm) knitting needles
Size F (3.75 mm) crochet hook
Approx. 15 matte blue 1/2" (1 cm) long bugle beads
Approx. 21 g blue 1/4" (.5 cm) drop beads
Approx. 14 g blue 1/8" (.25 cm) drop beads
Approx. 21 g blue/green size 8 seed beads
Beading thread in color to match yarn or beads
Beading needle

This project was made using the following yarn
S. Charles' Ritratto (28% mohair/53% viscose/10% polymide/9% polyester, 1.75oz/50g, 198yd/180m) 8 balls in color # 72 green and one ball in color #78 blue

Gauge in Stockinette Stitch
19 sts and 26 rows = 4" (10 cm)

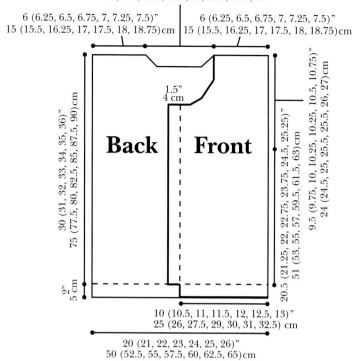

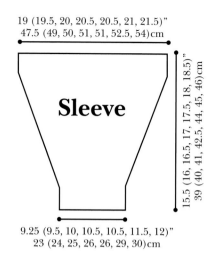

Back

Using the green yarn, CO 95 (100, 105, 109, 114, 119, 124) sts.

Work even in St st until piece measures 31 1/2 (32 1/2, 33 1/2, 34 1/2, 35 1/2, 36 1/2, 37 1/2)" / 79 (81, 84, 86, 89, 91, 94) cm.

On next right side row, k 32 (33, 34, 35, 36, 37, 38) sts, transfer center 31 (34, 37, 39, 42, 45, 48) sts to st holder, attach new ball of yarn and k rem 32 (33, 34, 35, 36, 37, 38) sts. Work ea side separately.

Purl 1 row.

Dec 1 st ea neck edge every right side row 3 times - 29 (30, 31, 32, 33, 34, 35) sts ea shoulder. BO.

Right Front

Using the green yarn, CO 48 (50, 52, 54, 57, 59, 62) sts. Work 12 rows in St st.

Knit next row then CO 8 sts for center band - 56 (58, 60, 62, 65, 67, 70) sts.

Purl next row. Continue in St st until piece measures 26 (27, 28, 29, 30, 31, 32)" / 65 (67.5, 70, 72.5, 75, 77.5, 80) cm.

On the next row beg at the center front BO 12 (13, 14, 15, 17, 18, 20) sts. Dec 1 st at the neck edge on every row 7 times, then every other row 8 times - 29 (30, 31, 32, 33, 34, 35) sts. Work even in St st until piece meas 32 (33, 34, 35, 36, 37, 38)" / 80 (82.5, 85, 87.5, 90, 92.5, 95) cm. BO.

Left Front

Using the green yarn, CO 48 (50, 52, 54, 57, 59, 62) sts. Beg on wrong side, purl first row.

Work 11 more rows in St st.

Purl next row then CO 8 sts for center band - 56 (58, 60, 62, 65, 67, 70) sts.

Continue in St st until piece measures 26 (27, 28, 29, 30, 31, 32)" / 65 (67.5, 70, 72.5, 75, 77.5, 80) cm.

On the next row beg at the center front BO 12 (13, 14, 15, 17, 18, 20) sts.

Dec 1 st at the neck edge on every row 7 times, then every other row 8 times - 29 (30, 31, 32, 33, 34, 35) sts. Work even in St st until piece meas 32 (33, 34, 35, 36, 37, 38)" / 80 (82.5, 85, 87.5, 90, 92.5, 95) cm. BO.

Sleeves (make two)

Using the green yarn, CO 44 (46, 48, 51, 51, 54, 56) sts.

Knit even in St st for 3 1/2 (3 1/2, 3 1/2, 4, 4, 4, 4 1/2)" / 9 (9, 9, 10, 10, 10, 11) cm.

Cont in St st, inc 1 st ea side every 3rd row, 23 times - 90 (92, 94, 97, 97, 100, 102) sts.

Work even in St st until piece meas 15 1/2 (16, 16 1/2, 17, 17 1/2, 18, 18 1/2)" / 39 (40, 41, 42.5, 44, 45, 46) cm. BO.

Assembly

Block all pieces to size. Sew front to back at shoulders. Center sleeve at shoulder seam and sew sleeves in place. Sew sleeve seam and front to back at sides. Fold the bottom 2" of the jacket to wrong side and sew in place. Fold the 8 sts at center front to the wrong side on the front pieces and sew in place. Using the green yarn, single crochet along the front and back neckline. Steam block all edges.

Embroidery

Using two strands of the blue yarn held tog as one, Swiss darn the triangle pattern to the right front of the jacket, beginning the pattern 10 to 12 sts in from the center front folded edge, and about 3 or 4 rows down from the neckline. Be careful to keep your tension as loose as the finished knitting.

Make a single dangle at the top point of each triangle by stringing 1 bugle bead, 1 size 8 seed bead, 1 drop bead and 1 size 8 seed bead, then passing back through the bugle bead.

To add beads along the edge of the sleeves *string 1 size 8 seed bead, 1 drop bead, 1 size 8 seed bead, then pass through the next knitted stitch along the edge. Repeat from asterisk all the way around the edge of the sleeve. For added strength pass through all the beads again then weave in the ends.

Work the same beading pattern on the neckline as you did on the sleeves exept alternate the large and small drop beads for each group of three beads.

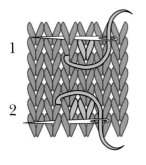

1

2

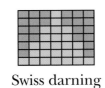

Swiss darning triangle pattern

dangle   bead edging

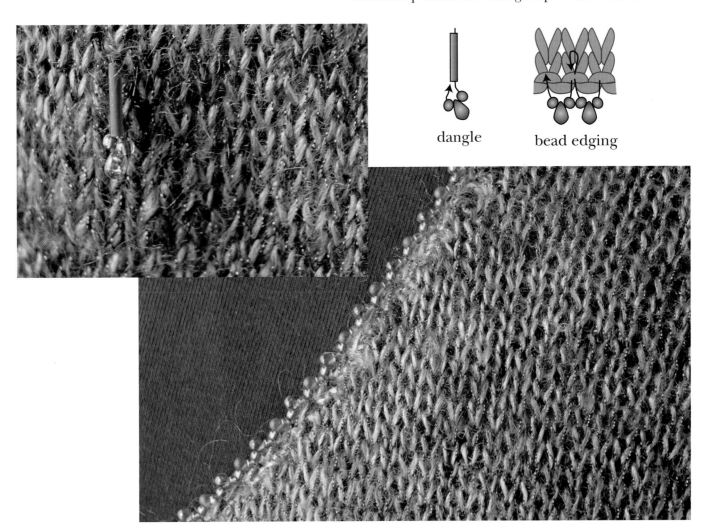

Silver Sweater Jacket

Here is an example of taking a color from your yarn to build your sweater design with details that are functional as well as decorative. The black beads and Swiss darned novelty yarn pull from the black in the metallic silver/black yarn, and the shell buttons pick up both colors. The bead edging not only enhances the design, the weight of the beads keep the Stockinette stitch edges from curling. And the crochet edging strengthens the neckline and becomes the buttonholes too!

Sizes
To fit bust sizes
36 (38, 40, 42, 44, 46, 48)"
    /90 (95, 100, 105, 110, 115, 120) cm

Knitted Measurements
Bust 38 (40, 42, 44, 46, 48, 50)"
    /95 (100, 105, 110, 115, 120, 125) cm
Length 21 1/2 (22, 22 1/2, 23, 23 1/2, 23 1/2, 24)"
    /54 (55, 56, 57.5, 59, 59, 60) cm
Upper Arm 12 1/2 (13, 13 1/2, 14, 14 1/2, 15, 16)"
    /31 (32.5, 34, 35, 36, 37.5, 40) cm

Materials
8 (8, 9, 9, 10, 11, 12) (.875oz/25g, 85yds/78m) balls
    metallic light worsted weight yarn in silver/ black 🌀4
Less than one ball (1.75oz/50g, 146yds/135m)
    eyelash novelty yarn in black 🌀4
Size 8 (5 mm) knitting needles at least 14" (35 cm) long
Size F crochet hook
5 3/4" (2 cm) buttons
Sewing needle and thread for buttons
Approx 1400 to 1800 size 8 black seed beads
Approx 200 to 250 black dagger beads (long pointed
drop beads)
Beading needle and beading thread

This project was made using the following yarn
6 skeins Berroco's Metallic FX (85% rayon/15% metallic,
.875oz/25g, 85yds/78m) color #1004 "Silver/Black" and
one ball of Crystal FX (100% nylon, 1.75oz/50g, 146yds/
135m) color #4734 "Patent Leather"

Gauge in Stockinette Stitch
22 sts and 30 rows = 4" (10 cm)

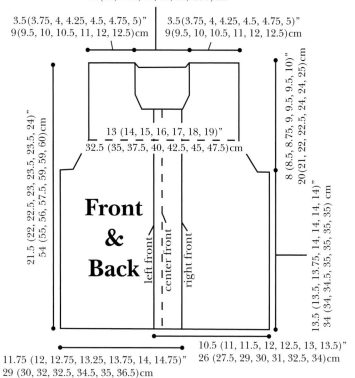

6(6.5, 7, 7.5, 8, 8.5, 9)"
15(16, 17.5, 19, 20, 21, 22.5)cm

3.5(3.75, 4, 4.25, 4.5, 4.75, 5)"
9(9.5, 10, 10.5, 11, 12, 12.5)cm

3.5(3.75, 4, 4.25, 4.5, 4.75, 5)"
9(9.5, 10, 10.5, 11, 12, 12.5)cm

13 (14, 15, 16, 17, 18, 19)"
32.5 (35, 37.5, 40, 42.5, 45, 47.5)cm

8 (8.5, 8.75, 9, 9.5, 9.5, 10)"
20(21, 22, 22.5, 24, 24, 25)cm

21.5 (22, 22.5, 23, 23.5, 23.5, 24)"
54 (55, 56, 57.5, 59, 59, 60)cm

Front & Back

left front
center front
right front

13.5 (13.5, 13.75, 14, 14, 14, 14)"
34 (34, 34.5, 35, 35, 35, 35) cm

10.5 (11, 11.5, 12, 12.5, 13, 13.5)"
26 (27.5, 29, 30, 31, 32.5, 34)cm

11.75 (12, 12.75, 13.25, 13.75, 14, 14.75)"
29 (30, 32, 32.5, 34.5, 35, 36.5)cm

19 (20, 21, 22, 23, 24, 25)"
47.5 (50, 52.5, 55, 57.5, 60, 62.5)cm

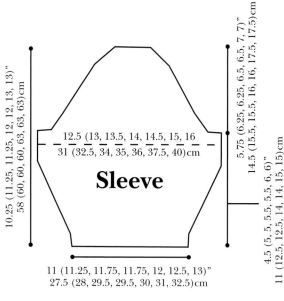

12.5 (13, 13.5, 14, 14.5, 15, 16
31 (32.5, 34, 35, 36, 37.5, 40)cm

Sleeve

10.25 (11.25, 11.25, 12, 12, 13, 13)"
58 (60, 60, 60, 63, 63, 63)cm

5.75 (6.25, 6.25, 6.5, 6.5, 7, 7)"
14.5 (15.5, 15.5, 16, 16, 17.5, 17.5)cm

4.5 (5, 5.5, 5.5, 5.5, 6, 6)"
11 (12.5, 12.5, 14, 14, 15, 15)cm

11 (11.25, 11.75, 11.75, 12, 12.5, 13)"
27.5 (28, 29.5, 29.5, 30, 31, 32.5)cm

Back

Using the silver yarn, CO 105 (110, 116, 121, 127, 132, 138) sts.

Work in St st until piece meas 13 1/2 (13 1/2, 13 3/4, 14, 14, 14, 14)" / 34 (34, 34.5, 35, 35, 35, 35) cm.

Armhole:
BO 5 sts at beg of next 2 rows - 95 (100, 106, 111, 117, 122, 128) sts.
Dec 1 st at ea end on every right side row 12 times - 71 (76, 82, 87, 93, 98, 104) sts.
Work even in St st until piece meas 21 (21 1/2, 22, 22 1/2, 23, 23, 23 1/2)"/ 52.5 (54, 55, 56, 57.5, 57.5, 59)cm.

Neck and Shoulders:
On next right side row, k 22 (23, 25, 26, 28, 29, 31) sts, transfer center 27 (30, 32, 35, 37, 40, 42) sts to st holder, attach new ball of yarn and k rem 22 (23, 25, 26, 28, 29, 31) sts.
Work ea side separately.
Purl 1 row.
Dec 1 st at neck edge every right side row 3 times - 19 (20, 22, 23, 25, 26, 28) sts ea shoulder.
At the same time BO 9 sts at the beg of armhole edge twice. BO rem sts.

Left Front

Using the silver yarn, CO 59 (61, 64, 67, 70, 72, 75) sts.
Work in St st until piece meas 13 1/2 (13 1/2, 13 3/4, 14, 14, 14, 14)" / 34 (34, 34.5, 35, 35, 35, 35) cm.

Armhole:
On the next row that beg at the armhole side, BO 5 sts - 54 (56, 59, 62, 65, 67, 70) sts.
Dec 1 st at armhole side every other row 12 times - 42 (44, 47, 50, 53, 55, 58) sts.

Neckline:
Work even in St st until piece meas 18 (18 1/4, 18 3/4, 19, 19, 19, 19)"/ 45 (45.5, 47, 47.5, 47.5, 47.5, 47.5) cm.
On the next row that beg at the center front, BO 13 (14, 15, 17, 18, 20, 21) sts.
Dec 1 st at the neck edge on every row 10 times - .
Work even in St st until piece meas 1/2" (1 cm) less than finished length.
On next two rows that beg at armhole side BO 9 sts.
BO rem sts.

Right Front

Using the silver yarn, CO 65 (67, 70, 73, 76, 78, 81) sts.
Work the same as the Left Front to the Neckline shaping.

Neckline shaping:
On the next row that beg at the center front, BO 19 (20, 21, 23, 24, 26, 27) sts.
Continue the same as for Left Front.

Sleeves (make two)

Using the silver yarn, CO 60 (62, 64, 64, 66, 69, 72) sts.

Knit even in St st for 4 rows.

Cont in St st, inc 1 st ea side every 6th (6th, 6th, 5th, 4th, 4th, 4th) row, 4 (5, 5, 6, 7, 7, 8) times - 68 (72, 74, 76, 80, 83, 88) sts.

Work even in St st until piece meas 4 1/2 (5, 5, 5 1/2, 5 1/2, 6, 6)" / 11 (12.5, 12.5, 14, 14, 15, 15) cm.

Shape cap:

BO 5 (5, 5, 5, 6, 6, 7) sts at beg of next 2 rows - 58 (62, 64, 66, 68, 71, 74) sts.

Dec 1 st at ea end every right side row 5 times, then every 3rd row 8 (9, 9, 10, 10, 11, 11) times, then every right side row 4 times. BO 4 sts at the beg of the next 2 rows.

BO rem 16 (18, 20, 20, 22, 23, 26) sts.

Assembly

Block all pieces. Sew front to back at shoulders. Center sleeve at shoulder seam and sew sleeves in place. Sew sleeve seam and front to back at sides. Fold 6 sts of the left center front to wrong side and sew in place. Fold 12 sts of right center front to wrong side and sew in place. Steam press along folds.

Neckband and Buttonholes

With right side of sweater facing you, using the crochet hook and silver yarn, single crochet around the edge of the neck and left front opening, making a 5-st chain and skipping 6 rows of knitting for ea buttonhole along the left center front fold. Space the buttonholes about 3 3/4" (10.5 cm) apart. Sew buttons to Right Front across from buttonholes, about 1" (2.5 cm) from the edge of the knitting.

Embroidery

Using the novelty yarn and tapestry needle, stitch the zigzag pattern on the lower front, back and sleeves of the sweater in Swiss darning, beginning the lowest stitch in the pattern 14 rows up from the bottom garment edge, and 8 rows up from the sleeve edge.

To stitch the bead pattern along the edges of the jacket, use the beading needle and beading thread, and begin with the thread coming out the end of one stitch along the edge of the sweater. String 4 size 8 seed beads, one dagger bead, 4 size 8 seed beads. Skip the next stitch on the knitted edge and pass the needle under the next stitch along the knitted edge. *Pass back through the last size 8 bead strung, string 3 size 8 seed beads, one dagger bead, 4 size 8 seed beads, skip the next stitch on the knitted edge and pass the needle under the next stitch on the knitted edge. Repeat from asterisk along the bottom edge of the jacket and the edges of the sleeves.

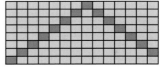

Swiss darning
zigzag pattern

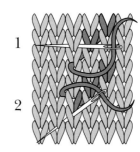

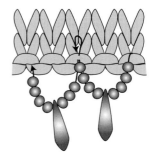

bead edging   **101**

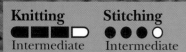

Knitting
■■■□ Intermediate

Stitching
●●●○ Intermediate

Red Sweater

This design uses easy stitch patterns and embroidery, with the same yarn the sweater is knit with, to bring out the best in the beautiful subtle variations of the hand dyed variegated yarn. The Swiss darning along the front panel is stitched using only the lightest colored sections of yarn, while the embroidered feather stitch uses the whole length of yarn so it moves through all the colors of the yarn, creating a texture more than a color design.

Sizes
To fit bust sizes
34 (36, 38, 40, 42, 44, 46)"
   /85 (90, 95, 100, 105, 110, 115) cm

Knitted Measurements
Bust 36 (38, 40, 42, 44, 46, 48)"
   /90 (95, 100, 105, 110, 115, 120) cm
Length 21 (22, 22 1/2, 23, 23 1/2, 24, 24)"
   /52.5 (55, 56, 57.5, 59, 60, 60) cm
Upper Arm 17 (17 1/2, 17 1/2, 18, 18, 18 1/2, 18 1/2)"
   /42.5 (44, 44, 45, 45, 46, 46) cm

Materials
4 (4, 4, 5, 5, 5, 6) (3.5oz/100g, 250yds/231m) skeins red
   and blue variegated worsted weight yarn 〔4〕
Size 7 (4.5 mm) knitting needles at least 14" (35 cm) long
Size 6 (4.25 mm) 32" circular knitting needles
Tapestry needle
Size G (4.5 mm) crochet hook

This project was made using the following yarn
4 skeins of Mountain Colors 4/8's wool (100% wool,
3.5oz/100g, 250yds/231m) color "Flathead cherry"

Gauge in Stockinette Stitch
20 sts and 30 rows = 4" (10 cm)

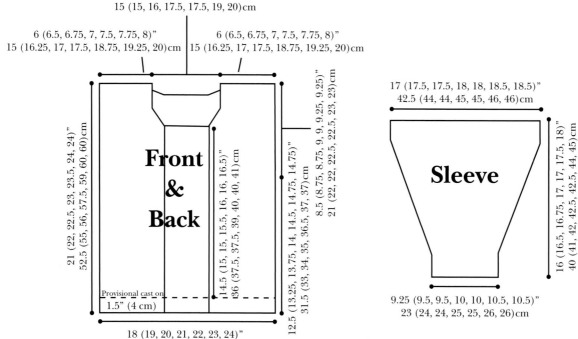

6 (6, 6.5, 7, 7, 7.5, 8)"
15 (15, 16, 17.5, 17.5, 19, 20)cm

6 (6.5, 6.75, 7, 7.5, 7.75, 8)"
15 (16.25, 17, 17.5, 18.75, 19.25, 20)cm

6 (6.5, 6.75, 7, 7.5, 7.75, 8)"
15 (16.25, 17, 17.5, 18.75, 19.25, 20)cm

21 (22, 22.5, 23, 23.5, 24, 24)"
52.5 (55, 56, 57.5, 59, 60, 60)cm

Front & Back

14.5 (15, 15, 15.5, 16, 16, 16.5)"
36 (37.5, 37.5, 39, 40, 40, 41)cm

8.5 (8.75, 8.75, 9, 9, 9.25, 9.25)"
21 (22, 22, 22.5, 22.5, 23, 23)cm

12.5 (13.25, 13.75, 14, 14.5, 14.75, 14.75)"
31.5 (33, 34, 35, 36.5, 37, 37)cm

Provisional cast on
1.5" (4 cm)

18 (19, 20, 21, 22, 23, 24)"
45 (47.5, 50, 52.5, 55, 57.5, 60)cm

17 (17.5, 17.5, 18, 18, 18.5, 18.5)"
42.5 (44, 44, 45, 45, 46, 46)cm

Sleeve

16 (16.5, 16.75, 17, 17, 17.5, 18)"
40 (41, 42, 42.5, 42.5, 44, 45)cm

9.25 (9.5, 9.5, 10, 10, 10.5, 10.5)"
23 (24, 24, 25, 25, 26, 26)cm

Back

Using the larger size needles CO 90 (96, 100, 105, 110, 115, 120) sts using a provisional cast on.

Work in St st until piece meas 19 (20, 20 1/2, 21, 21 1/2, 22, 22)"/ 47.5 (50, 51, 52.5, 54, 55, 55) cm.

On next right side row, k 31 (34, 36, 37, 39, 41, 43) sts, attach a new length of yarn, BO next 28 (28, 28, 31, 32, 33, 34) sts and knit rem k 31 (34, 36, 37, 39, 41, 43) sts.

Working ea side separately, dec one st at neck edge twice - 29 (32, 34, 35, 37, 39, 41) sts. BO.

Front

Side panels (make 2):

CO 33 (36, 38, 39, 41, 43, 45) sts using a provisional cast on.

Work in St st until piece measures 14 1/2 (15, 15, 15 1/2, 16, 16, 16 1/2)" / 36 (37.5, 37.5, 39, 40, 40, 41) cm.

Cont in St st dec 1 st at center front every 4th row 4 times - 29 (32, 34, 35, 37, 39, 41) sts.

Work even in St st until piece meas 19 1/2 (20 1/2, 21, 21 1/2, 22, 22, 22 1/2)"/ 52.5 (55, 56, 57.5, 59, 60, 60) cm. BO.

Center Front Panel

CO 72 (75, 75, 78, 80, 80, 83) sts.

Work in St st for 31 (31, 31, 33, 33, 37, 37) rows.

BO.

Sleeves (make 2)

CO 46 (48, 48, 50, 50, 52, 52) sts.

Work in Garter st for 3 rows.

Work in Seed st for 6 rows.

Work in St st, inc 1 st ea side every 5th row, 19 (20, 20, 20, 20, 20, 20) times - 84 (88, 88, 90, 90, 92, 92) sts.

Work even in St st until piece meas 16(16 1/2, 16 3/4, 17, 17, 17 1/2, 18)" / 40 (41, 42, 42 1/2, 42 1/2, 44, 45)cm. BO.

Assembly

Sew front side panels to center front panel, matching bottom edges and top of center panel to side panels before decreases. Sew front to back at shoulders. Center sleeve over shoulder seam and sew in place. Sew sleeve and side seams.

Bottom and neck edges

With right side of sweater facing you, using the smaller size needles, pick up and knit all provisional cast on stitches from front and back and 26 (26, 26, 28, 28, 31, 31) sts from the bottom of the center front panel - 182 (194, 202, 211, 220, 232, 241) sts.

Working in the round, work 6 rows in Seed st and 3 rows in Garter st. BO.

Single crochet around neck edging.

Embroidery

Following the graphs below, Swiss darn the repeat pattern down the front of the center panel, beginning 2 (2, 2, 3, 3, 4, 4) rows in from the edges of the panel and using only lengths of the brightest color of the variegated yarn. Beginning with the yarn coming out 1 stitch down, and 2 rows to the left of the center of the top of the center panel, embroider the center panel with double feather stitch as shown below.

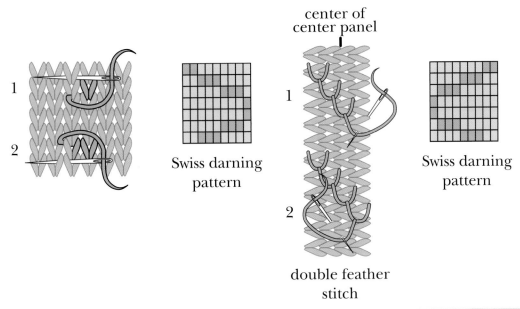

Swiss darning pattern

center of center panel

Swiss darning pattern

double feather stitch

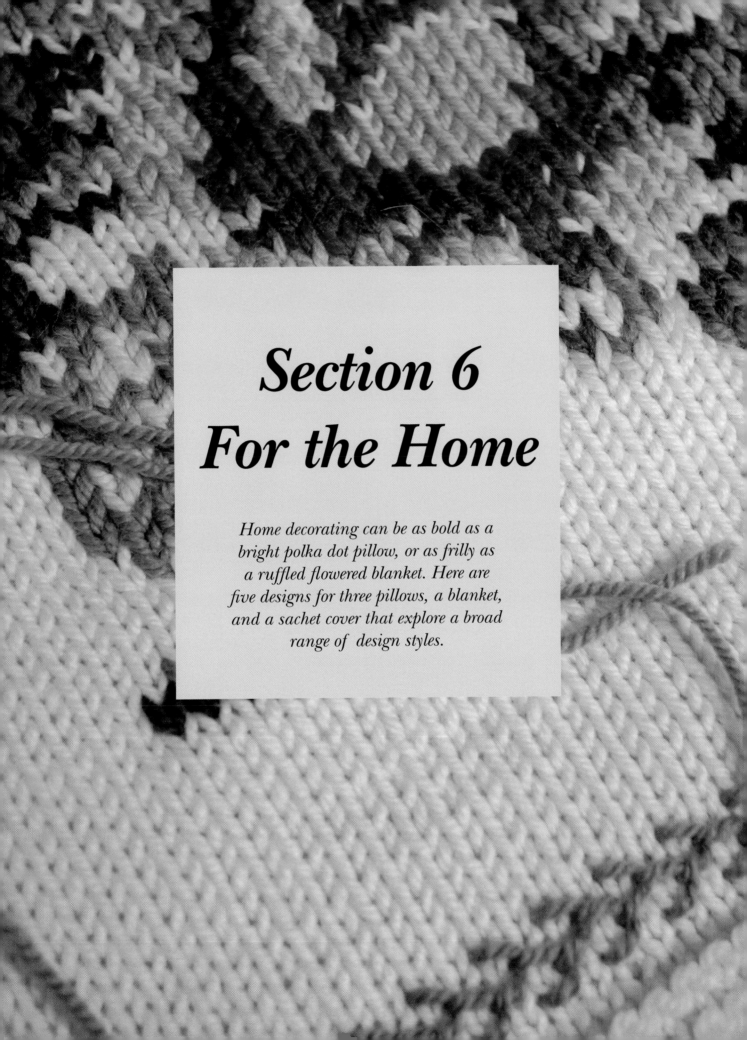

Section 6
For the Home

Home decorating can be as bold as a bright polka dot pillow, or as frilly as a ruffled flowered blanket. Here are five designs for three pillows, a blanket, and a sachet cover that explore a broad range of design styles.

Knitting
Beginner

Stitching
● ○ ○ ○
Beginner

Easy Polka-Dot Pillow

This easy to knit pillow is simply a Stockinette stitch rectangle folded in half. The brightly colored Swiss darned polka dots are a great way to try out the stitch to see if you like it. You can stitch them before you sew the pillow together, or on the finished pillow as I did.

Finished size
20" (50 cm) square

Materials
3 skeins (3.5oz/100g, 183yd/169m each) of teal worsted weight yarn (4)
1 skein (1.75oz/50g, 198yd/180m) of pink lace weight metallic yarn (2)
Size 9 (5.5 mm) 24" circular knitting needles
Size 20" (50 cm) square pillow form
Tapestry needle

This project was made using the following yarn
Tahki Yarns' Donegal Tweed (100% pure new wool, 3.5oz/100g, 183yd/169m) color #809 teal and S. Charles' Ritratto (28% mohair/53% viscose/10% polymide/9% polyester, 1.75oz/50g, 198yd/180m) color # 77 pink

Gauge in Stockinette Stitch
14 sts and 20 rows = 4" (10 cm)

Pillow
Using the worsted weight yarn, CO 68 sts.
Work in St st until piece measures 40" (1 m) long.
BO.

Assembly
Fold in half to a 20" (50 cm) square.
Using mattress stitch, sew the two sides together and about 2" (5 cm) at each corner of last side. Insert pillow form. Sew remaining section of last side closed.

Embroidery
Using three strands of the lace weight yarn held tog as one and the tapestry needle, follow the chart, Swiss darning polka dots randomly spaced 2" (5 cm) to 4" (10 cm) apart on the front of the pillow. Weave in ends.

Seam together along 2 sides and part of last side near corners.

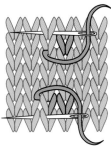

Swiss darning stitch

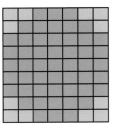

Polka dot chart

Knitting
■□□□
Beginner

Stitching
●●○○
Easy

Fuzzy Wave Bolster Pillow

Here's another easy to knit project which is just a rectangle gathered at the ends and seamed together along the side. The novelty yarn can be a little tricky to stitch, but if you are careful to hold the yarn out of the way as you pull your stitches through, the stitching will go smoothly. Making the long stitches helps the stitching go fast and allows the fuzzy yarn to fluff up and show off it's true character.

Finished size
16" (40 cm) long by 6" (15 cm) diameter

Materials
4 balls (3.5oz/100g, 163yd/150m) of brown dk weight yarn (3)
2 balls (1.75/50g, 77yd/70m) of brown novelty eyelash yarn (4)
Size 9 (5.5 mm) knitting needles at least 14" (35 cm) long
16" (40 cm) long by 6" (15 cm) diameter pillow form
Tapestry needle

This project was made using the following yarn
Patons' Katrina (92% rayon/8% polyester, 3.5oz/ 100g, 163yd/150m) color #10031 "Chocolate" and Cha Cha (100% nylon, 1.75/50g, 77yd/70m) color #02018 "Soul"

Gauge in Stockinette Stitch
19 sts and 30 rows = 4" (10 cm)

Pillow
Using the dk weight yarn, CO 82 sts.
Work in Stockinette stitch until piece measures 22" (55 cm) long. Cut the working yarn 10" (25 cm) from the last st, thread with the tapestry needle and pass through remaining stitches, pulling the last row into a tightly gathered circle. Weave in end. Pass another 10" (25 cm) length of yarn through the cast on stitches and pull into a tight circle. Weave in end. Insert the pillow form and sew the side seam with mattress stitch. Weave in ends.

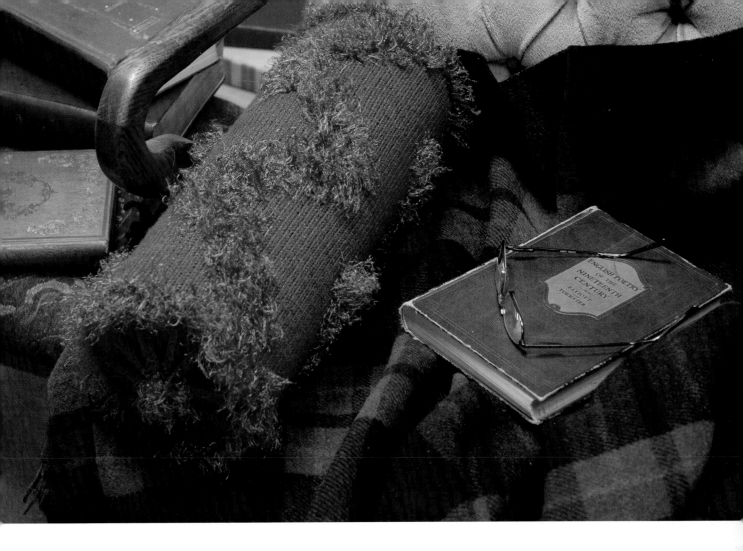

Embroidery

Follow the pattern for the elongated Swiss darning stitches, working 8 long stitches over 6 rows of knitting and skipping a row between groups of stitches, offsetting each group by 4 stitches, creating the zig-zag pattern. Skip 20 stitches along the top row and make another zig-zag stripe. Repeat once more, so you have 3 zig-zag stripes around the pillow.

To make the edging, make elongated Swiss darning stitches over 4 rows all along the edges and straight stitch over the hole at each end. Fluff up the novelty yarn by lightly scraping a knitting needle over the finished stitches to pull up the fluff.

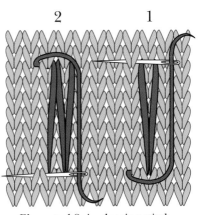

Elongated Swiss darning stitch

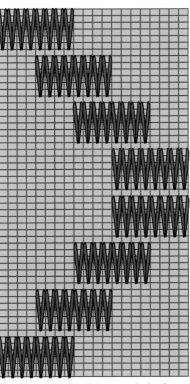

Elongated Swiss darning stitch chart

111

Knitting
◼◼◼▯
Intermediate

Stitching
●●●○
Intermediate

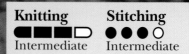

Gardenia Pillow

Here is a pillow with a variety of details and design options. You can knit it completely, sew it to a purchased pillow, or sew it to a pillow you make yourself. The pillow section is easy since it is just a tube gathered together at one end. Knit the flower in one piece using short rows to complete the petals one by one, then spiral the petals together to create the flower.

Finished size
16" (40 cm) round pillow with 4" (10 cm) sewn fabric ruffle and backing (shown), or 18" (45 cm) round pillow knitted front and back without a ruffle or rolled edge.

Materials
2 balls (3.5oz/100g, 150yd/138m) tan worsted weight yarn ⓸

1 ball each (3.5oz/100g, 150yd/138m) cream and pale green worsted weight yarn ⓸

Size 9 (5.5 mm) 32" (80 cm) circular needles

Tapestry needle

Stitch marker

16" (40 cm) circular pillow form

1 1/2 yds of cotton fabric to match dark tan yarn

5 yds of size 5 or 8 pearl cotton, any color

Sewing machine

Sewing needle and thread to match fabric

This project was made using the following yarn
Blue Sky Alpacas, Inc. Blue Sky Organic Cotton (100% organic cotton, 3.5oz/100g, 150yd/138m) 2 balls of color #82 "Nut" (tan), 1 ball each of color #83 "Sage" (pale green) and #80 "Bone" (cream)

Gauge in Stockinette Stitch
16 sts and 21 rows = 4" (10 cm)

Note
To make this pillow without the fabric backing, you will need 4 balls of the tan yarn and an 18" (45 cm) pillow form instead of a 16" (40 cm) pillow form. Omit fabric sewing machine, sewing needle and thread and pearl cotton.

Pillow (Make 1 for 16" (40 cm) fabric-backed pillow. Make 2 for 18" (45 cm) knitted pillow front and back)
Using the tan yarn, CO 190 sts, join into a circle, pm.
Working in the round, knit in St st for 36 rounds.
Round 37: K2tog, rep around – 95 sts.
Round 38: K2tog, rep to last st, k 1 – 48 sts.
Cut yarn to 18" (45 cm), thread with tapestry needle and pass through all sts. Pull tight so there is about a 1" (2.5 cm) hole in the center of the gathers. Secure the thread and weave in end.

Making the Ruffled Fabric Pillow - use 1/2" (1 cm) seams throughout (Do not make for 18" pillow)
Cut the fabric into two 17" (43 cm) circles and four 9" (23 cm) strips the width of the fabric. Seam the strips tog at the short ends creating a tube. Fold the long sides of the fabric tube in half, right sides tog so you have a 4 1/2" (11 cm) wide tube. Zigzag stitch 1/4" (.5 cm) from the raw edges, encasing the pearl cotton in the stitching, but not piercing it as you sew. Pull both ends of the pearl cotton, gathering the tube into a ruffle. Pin in place on the right side of one of the 17" (43 cm) circles matching the raw edges and adjusting the ruffles until they are even. Sew in place through all layers 1/2" (1 cm) from the edge. Pin the remaining 17" (43 cm) circle, right sides tog, over the ruffled circle. Seam together, leaving a 12" opening. Turn right sides out, insert the pillow form and and sew the 12" opening closed.

Leaves (Make 5)
Using the green yarn, CO 1 st.
Row 1: K into front and back of st – 2 sts.
Row 2: P into front and back of st, p1 –3 sts.
Row 3: K into front and back of st, k2 – 4 sts.
Row 4: P into front and back of st, p3 – 5 sts.
Continuing in St st, rep inc at beg of ea row until you have 15 sts.
Work even in St st for 10 rows.
Cut yarn to 8" (20 cm) and transfer leaf to a spare needle.
Repeat for each leaf, placing them all on the same needle as shown at right.
Knit across all the stitches.
Cut yarn to 10" (25 cm), thread with tapestry needle and pass through all sts. Set aside.

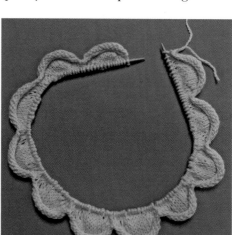

Gardenia (Make 1)
Using the white yarn, CO 165 sts.
One petal:
Row 1: K15, turn.
Row 2: Sl 1, p13, turn.
Row 3: Sl 1, k12, turn.
Row 4: Sl 1, p11, turn.
Row 5: Sl 1, k10, turn.
Row 6: Sl 1, p9, turn.
Row 7: Sl 1, k8, turn.
Row 8: Sl 1, p7, turn.
Row 9: Sl 1, k6, turn.
Row 10: Sl 1, p5, turn.
Row 11: Sl 1, k9, do not turn.
Repeat rows 1-11 on each group of 15 sts until you reach the other end of the cast on sts.
You will have 165 sts and 11 petals as shown above right.
Purl across all sts.
Cut yarn to 24" (58 cm), thread with tapestry needle and pass through all sts.

Constructing the Gardenia

Beginning with the petal last exited, roll the knitting into a tight spiral, stitching the base of the petals in place with the 24" (58 cm) length of yarn as you arrange the petals around the first center petal. To do this, take a stitch in the second petal (1), then take a stitch in the first petal (2), then take a stitch in the third petal (3) then take a stitch in the in the first petal again. Continue stitching in each next petal (4), then in the growing flower (5), until you've sewn all the petals around the first petal (6).

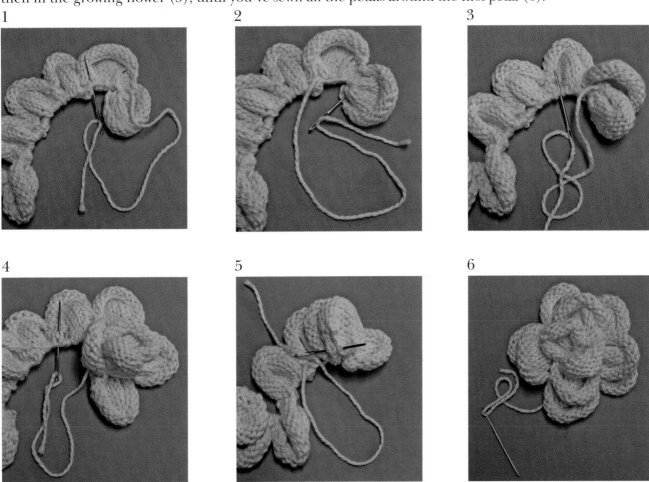

Assembly

Using the sewing needle and thread, back stitch the knitted pillow top to the front of the pillow, stitching about 1" (2.5 cm) from the edge of the knitting, so the edge curls over. Use the remaining tail of the flower and the tapestry needle, attach the flower to the center of the knitted pillow front, covering the 1" (2.5 cm) hole in the center. Arrange the leaves around base of the flower on the pillow top and sew in place using the remaining tail of the leaves and the tapestry needle.

Optional 18" Pillow knitted front and back without fabric ruffle

Make two pillow pieces, and the leaves and gardenia the same as for the ruffled pillow. Hand seam the front and back pillow pieces together along the edges using the tan yarn and tapestry needle, inserting the pillow form when you have sewn about two thirds around the edge. Add flower and petal as described above.

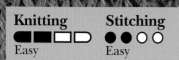

Knitting
■■□▭
Easy

Stitching
●●○○
Easy

Fair Isle Style Pillow

Fair Isle knitting is a beautiful technique with intricate details in color changes and patterns. To make this Fair Isle pillow without the more complicated Fair Isle technique, you'll knit only a pattern of stripes, then when the knitting is through, you Swiss darn the detailed color patterned repeats across the stripes.

Finished size
18" (45 cm) square

Materials
2 skeins each (1.75oz/50g, 109yd/101m) sport
   weight yarn in medium green, yellowgreen, blue,
   lavender, purple, gray and white ⟨2⟩
Size 7 (4.5 mm) knitting needles at least 14" (35 cm)
   long
18" (45 cm) square pillow form
Two 19" (47.5 cm) squares of backing fabric
Tapestry needle
Straight pins
Sewing needle and thread to match fabric
Sewing Machine (optional)

This project was made using
Classic Elite's Inca Alpaca (100% alpaca, 1.75oz/
50g, 109yd/101m) 2 skeins each in colors #1135
"Cala Cala Moss" (medium green), #1197 "Canyon
Green" (yellowgreen), #1146 "Island of the Sun"
(blue), #1131 "Blue Danube" (lavender), #1154
"Purple Haze" (purple), #1176 "Gaucho Grey
Heather" (gray), and #1116 "Natural" (white)

Gauge in Stockinette Stitch
17 sts and 22 rows = 4" (10 cm)

Pillow
Begining with the blue yarn, CO 78 sts.
Knitting in Stockinette stitch, follow the color
pattern on the facing page once from bottom to top,
then once more up to the asterisk (*). BO in blue.
Block to 19" (47.5 cm) square.

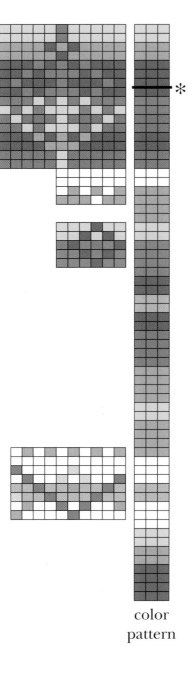

color
pattern

Assembly

Place the knitting and one backing fabric square right sides together. Place the remaining backing fabric square over the knitting, right side toward the knitting. Pin together around edges. Machine or hand sew 1/2" (1 cm) seam allowance along three sides of the pieces and part of the last side as shown. Trim corners of fabric and turn right side out. Insert pillow form and hand stitch remaining side closed.

Embroidery

Swiss darn the repeat patterns over the stripes following chart above. For the tree pattern, center the first tree in the middle of the stripe on the pillow, then stitch the other two trees beginning 8 stitches away to the right and left.

117

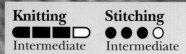
Sachet Pillow

A beautiful colored yarn, a scrap of fabric,- and some beads are all you need to make this delicate sachet holder. First choose the center accent bead, then find all the other beads to go with the yarn color or accent bead. Making the sachet with an overlapping ribbed closure on the back creates a versatile sachet holder which can be used over and over again. The fabric on the inside makes the beads stay in place.

Finished size
5 1/2" by 6 1/2" / (14 cm by 16 cm)

Materials
1/2 skein (1.75oz/50g, 146yd/133m) of pale green sport weight
  yarn **②**
Size 3 (3 mm) knitting needles at least 8" (20 cm) long
60 to 70 size 8 cream seed beads
Nine 3/16" (4 mm) long side drilled drop beads
Approx. 20 to 25 1/4" (6 mm) long pearl cream bugle beads
Approx. 20 size 11 cream seed beads
One 1/2" (13 mm) wide accent bead
Beading needle and thread to match yarn
Tapestry needle
5" (12.5 cm) square cotton fabric

This project was made using the following yarn
Blue Sky Alpacas' Alpaca & Silk (50% superfine alpaca/50% silk,
.75oz/50g, 146yd/133m) color #i16 "Spring"

Gauge in Stockinette Stitch
29 sts and 35 rows = 4" (10 cm)

Front
CO 40 sts.
Row 1: (K1, p1) repeat across.
Row 2: (P1, k1) repeat across.
Repeat rows 1 and 2 twice more (6 rows total in seed st).
Row 7: (K1, p1) twice, k to last 5 sts, (p1, k1) twice, p1.
Row 8: (P1, k1) twice, p to last 5 sts, (k1, p1) twice, k1.
Repeat rows 7 and 8 twenty-one times (42 rows total).
Repeat rows 1 and 2 three times (6 rows of seed st), BO.

Back (make two)
CO 30 sts.
Row 1: (K2, p2) repeat to last 2 sts, k2.
Row 2: (P2, k2) repeat to last 2 sts, p2.
Repeat rows 1 and 2 three more times - 8 rows total. Work in Stockinette stitch for 18 rows, BO.

Embroidery

Center the fabric on the backside of the front piece and pin in place. Using the beading needle and beading thread, and working through both layers on the front side of the knitting, locate the center of the knitting and sew the accent bead in place. Stitch the size 11 beads around the accent bead. Stitch the bugle beads radiating out from the size 11 beads. Sew three drop beads at the top, bottom and sides of the circle of bugle beads. Sew size 8 seed beads randomly over the remaining surface of the St st portion of the knitting, spacing them about 1/2" (1 cm) apart.

Assembly

Trim the excess fabric from the backside of the embroidered knitting so that the fabric is within the Stockinette Stitch section of knitting. Using the tapestry needle and a strand of yarn, sew one back piece to the back of the embroidered piece along the edge of the Stockinette stitch section of the knitting, matching the pieces up stitch for stitch and row for row. Repeat with the other back piece, overlapping the first back-piece by about 12 rows.

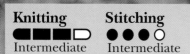

Knitting
Intermediate

Stitching
Intermediate

Ruffled Rose Blanket

This warm and cozy blanket is made in sections and then sewn together, with the ruffle added at the end. You can stitch the embroidery after the blanket is complete, or embroider the blocks before assembly. Just the center block has the Swiss darned rose pattern, but you could choose to stitch the same pattern in every other block or every block for a colorful detailed design.

Finished size
44" (110 cm) square

Materials
20 balls (1.75oz/50g, 90yds/82m) cream colored worsted weight yarn 4
1 ball each (1.75oz/50g, 90yds/82m) worsted weight yarn in maroon, rose, pink, cornflower, dark green, turquoise, medium green, yellow, pale blue, lavender, and deep purple 4
Size 9 (5.5 mm) 32" (80 cm) circular knitting needles
Stitch holders
Stitch markers
Tapestry needle

This project was made using the following yarn
Jaeger Matchmaker Merino Aran (100% merino wool, 1.75oz/50g, 90yds/82m) 20 balls of color #662 "Cream" and one ball each of colors #769 "Prose" (maroon), #756 "Mulberry" (rose), #773 "Wild Rose" (pink), #629 "Mariner" (cornflower), #730 "Loden" (dark green), #754 "Eucalyptus" (turquoise), #755 "Sage" (medium green), #762 "Glow" (yellow), #770 "Ice" (pale blue), #772 "Clover" (lavender), #775 "Gloxinia" (deep purple)

Gauge in Stockinette Stitch
16 sts and 22 rows = 4" (10 cm)

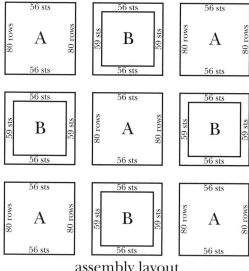

assembly layout

Stockinette Stitch Panel "A" (make 5)

Using the cream yarn, CO 56 sts with a provisional cast on. Work in St st for 80 rows. Move to stitch holder, set aside.

Garter Stitch Edged Panel "B" (make 4)

Using the cream yarn, CO 50 sts with a provisional cast on. Work in St st for 70 rows.

Garter Stitch Border

Continuing on next row, k across, pm, do not turn - 50 sts.
Working along the left side, pick up and k 3 sts for every 4 rows of knitting 17 times (68 rows), pick up and k 1 st for ea of the next 2 rows, pm - 53 sts.
Working along the bottom edge, pick up and k provisional cast on, pm - 50 sts.
Working along the right side, pick up and k 3 sts for every 4 rows of knitting 17 times (68 rows), pick up and k 1 st for ea of the next 2 rows, pm - 53 sts, 206 sts total.
Work in the round for the remainder of the panel.
Rnd 1: Purl ea st.
Rnd 2: Inc 1 in ea st before and after marker, k all other sts - 8 sts increased, 52 on top and bottom, 55 on sides, 214 total.
Rep rnd 1 and 2 twice more (6 rows, 56 sts along ea top and bottom edge and 59 sts along ea side edge - 230 sts total). Thread all sts on scrap of yarn, set aside.

122

Assembly (Swiss darning embroidery can be stitched before or after assembly)
Arrange three panels vertically A-B-A. Graft tog. Repeat for another set of panels. Arrange rem panels vertically B-A-B and graft tog. Sew the three-panel strips tog along sides in mattress stitch, matching the corners of the panels.

Ruffled edge (Work each side separately then seam tog at corners in mattress st.)

Top and bottom:
Row 1: With right side facing, pick up and k each st along one side of blanket – 168 sts.
Row 2 – 5: Beg on a wrong side row, work in seed st, increasing one st at ea end on every right side row – 172 sts.
Row 6: Purl.
Row 7: K into front and back of ea st across – 344 sts.
Row 8: Purl.
Row 9 – 11: Knit.
Row 12 – 13: Purl.
BO.

Sides:
Row 1: With right side facing, pick up and k 3 sts for every 4 rows along first block (60 sts), all 59 sts on middle block, and 3 sts for every 4 rows on last block (60 sts) - 179 sts.
Work the same as the top and bottom sections for the remainder of the ruffle - 181 sts after row 3, 183 sts after row 5, 366 sts after row 7.

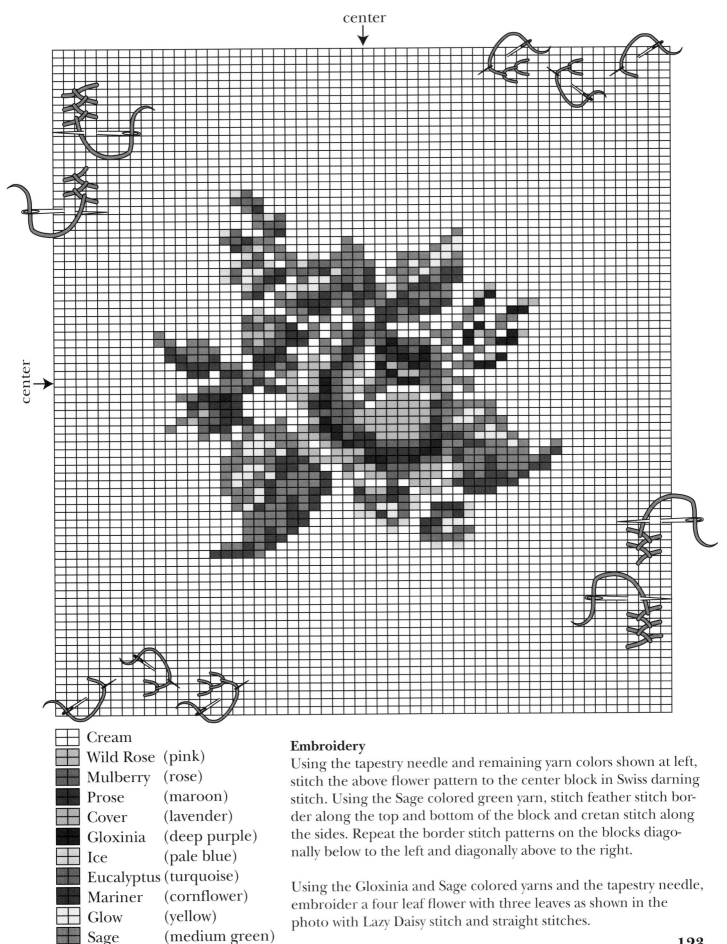

center

center

☐	Cream
▨	Wild Rose (pink)
▨	Mulberry (rose)
■	Prose (maroon)
▨	Cover (lavender)
■	Gloxinia (deep purple)
▨	Ice (pale blue)
▨	Eucalyptus (turquoise)
▨	Mariner (cornflower)
☐	Glow (yellow)
▨	Sage (medium green)
▨	Loden (dark green)

Embroidery

Using the tapestry needle and remaining yarn colors shown at left, stitch the above flower pattern to the center block in Swiss darning stitch. Using the Sage colored green yarn, stitch feather stitch border along the top and bottom of the block and cretan stitch along the sides. Repeat the border stitch patterns on the blocks diagonally below to the left and diagonally above to the right.

Using the Gloxinia and Sage colored yarns and the tapestry needle, embroider a four leaf flower with three leaves as shown in the photo with Lazy Daisy stitch and straight stitches.

123

Glossary

Appliqué - Attaching a separate piece of material to the surface of a project either with small stitches along the edge of the piece so that they don't show, or with decorative stitches such as buttonhole stitch.

Back stitch - A line of stitching worked from right to left, by making a small stitch on the top of the fabric, inserting the needle a stitch length to the right and coming back up through the fabric two stitch lengths to the left. Can be decorative or functional.

Beading needle - A needle, thin enough to string beads, with an eye large enough to thread beading thread. The most common beading needle is 2" long in sizes 16 (very thin) to size 10 (largest), and is sharp at the end. There is also a shorter needle for bead embroidery that is blunt ended.

Blind hem stitch - A functional stitch used in appliqué to sew the edges of a piece of fabric down to the base fabric. A very small stitch is made on the front of the piece through all thicknesses and then thread is carried along the backside a short distance. This is repeated around the appliqué.

Block or blocking - to dampen or steam dampen a piece of knitting, shape it into desired dimensions, then leave to dry.

Beading thread - Strong thin thread used specifically for beadwork, including brands such as Nymo nylon filament thread and Sylamide thread. Fine silk thread is also used for beading.

Blunt ended - When the pointed end of a needle is rounded as in a tapestry needle.

Chain stitch - An embroidery stitch resembling a chain in which loops of thread are worked in a line on the surface of the fabric, each one caught in the previous loop.

Chenille needle - A large needle with a sharp pointed end and a large eye. Used with yarn and decorative threads for embroidery when you want to pierce fabric, rather than passing through holes in canvas, or between fabric threads.

Cretan stitch - An embroidery stitch which creates a line of offset opposing vertical stitches, each one catching the yarn or thread as the stitch is pulled in place.

Cube bead - A bead shaped like a box or cube. The hole can go through the center of the box shape, or it can pass through the box shape diagonally from corner to corner.

Dangle - A strand of beads attached to a project at one end of the strand so the other end dangles. Fringe is made of many dangles.

Diamond smocking stitch - An embroidery stitch in smocking made of two rows of stitching which zigzag alternately gathering the fabric horizontally, creating a diamond pattern over the two rows.

Double feather stitch - A variation of feather stitch in which the loops of thread are worked several times in one direction, then they are worked several times in the other direction.

Drop bead - A bead resembling a drop of liquid. It is narrow at one end and wide at the other, with the bead hole passing horizontally through the narrow end of the drop shape.

Duplicate stitch (also known as Swiss darning) - An embroidery stitch used on knitted garments in which you duplicate the knitted stitches by embroidering over them in another color, following the same path as the knitted yarn.

Elongated Swiss darning stitch - A variation of Swiss darning stitch in which the same pattern of the Swiss darning stitch is worked over two or more rows of knitting for each stitch.

Embellishment - To add decorative detail to something.

Embroidery - To decorate a surface with decorative stitching.

Faceted bead - A bead ground flat on one or more sides creating facets that sparkle when they reflect the light.

Fern stitch - An embroidery stitch repeated to form a line, made of a "V" shaped stitch, tacked in place at the bottom of the "V" with a small stitch.

Feather stitch - An embroidery stitch made of interlocking loops shaped like a "U" with each new loop beginning at the base of the previous "U" and offset by half a stitch width, alternating to the right and then to the left for each new stitch.

Feathered chain stitch - A zigzag line of embroidery made of lazy daisy chain stitches, with elongated straight stitches arranged at alternating right angles.

Fly stitch - An isolated embroidery stitch made of a "V" shaped stitch, tacked in place at the bottom of the "V" with a small stitch.

Fringe - A group of dangles of beads or strands of yarn attached to a project.

Gauge - The number of stitches and rows in a measured area of knitting. Matching this measurement ensures your project will be the same size as stated in the instructions.

Herringbone stitch - An embroidery stitch with alternating slanting stitches that overlap along a row of stitching.

Lazy daisy stitch - An embroidery stitch made of a loop of thread with the loop held in place with a small tacking stitch.

Leaf bead - A bead made in the shape of a leaf. The hole can go through the center of the the leaf from end to end, through the base of the bead from side to side, or through the base of the bead from front to back.

Mattress stitch - A functional stitch commonly used to sew knitted garment pieces together in which both pieces are butted up edge to edge, then a stitch is taken alternately on one piece and then on the other. Every few stitches, the thread is pulled tightly to hide the seam.

Satin stitch - An embroidery stitch made of straight stitches lined up next to each other to fill a shape with color.

Seed bead - A small rounded bead ranging in size from about 1/4" (5 mm), size 5 to less than 1/16" (1.5 mm), size 15.

Smocking - An embroidery technique in which pleated fabric is decoratively stitched to hold the pleats in place. Alternatively, smocking can gather the fabric as you stitch, which is the method for the project in this book.

Stem stitch - An embroidery stitch made of overlapping straight stitches in which a long stitch is taken on the front of the fabric, then the needle is brought up just to one side (always the same side) of the middle of the long stitch. The long stitch on the top and the short stitch underneath are repeated, forming a line of stitching.

Stitch length - The length of a single stitch on the top of the fabric.

Straight stitch - An isolated embroidery stitch made of a simple stitch, long or short in any direction.

Stretched fly stitch - A variation of fly stitch in which the small tacking stitch is made as long as the legs of the "V" shape of the stitch and linked together forming a fern shaped pattern.

Swiss darning (Also known as duplicate stitch) - An embroidery stitch used on knitted garments in which you duplicate the knitted stitches by embroidering over them in another color, following the same path as the knitted yarn.

Tapestry needle - A large needle with a blunt end, used for sewing seams in knitting and crochet, and for needlepoint and canvas embrodery.

Tension - In knitting and embroidery, the tightness or looseness of stitches.

Threaded back stitch - An embroidery stitch in which a row of back stitch is made, then another thread is passed behind the back stitches using a blunt needle, alternately passing behind from below one stitch then from above the next stitch.

Threaded herringbone stitch - An embroidery stitch in which a row of herringbone stitch is made, then another thread is passed behind the center of the herringbone stitches using a blunt needle, alternately passing behind from below one stitch then from above the next stitch.

Whipped chain stitch - An embroidery stitch in which a row of chain stitch is made, then another thread is passed behind each loop of the chain using a blunt needle, always passing in the same direction for each stitch.

Supply Sources

Here are the yarn companies whose yarn was used for projects in this book. Some are wholesale only, but you can check their web pages to find stores that carry their products.

Bernat, Patons and Lily Yarns
P.O. Box 40
Listowel, Ontario,
Canada N4W 3H3
www.patonsyarns.com
- Cowlneck Sweater, pg. 78
- Fuzzy Wave Bolster Pillow, pg. 110

Berroco, Inc.
P.O. Box 367
14 Elmdale Road
Uxbridge, MA 01569
www.berroco.com
- Black Swirls Wrap, pg. 36
- Purple Suede Sweater, pg. 66
- Silver Sweater Jacket, pg 98

Brown Sheep Co., Inc.
100662 County Road 16
Mitchell, NE 69357
www.brownsheep.com
- Triangles Hat, pg. 22
- Falling Leaves Sweater, pg. 62

Blue Sky Alpacas, Inc.
PO Box 387
St. Francis, MN 55070
www.blueskyalpacas.com
- Big Yarn Hats, pg. 20
- Celtic Diamonds Scarf, pg. 38
- Gardenia Pillow, pg. 112
- Sachet Pillow, pg. 118

Cascade Yarns
1224 Andover Park E
Tukwila, WA 98188
www.cascadeyarns.com
- Woodland Scarf, pg. 34
- Pretty in Pink Tank, pg. 82

Classic Elite Yarns
122 Western Ave.
Lowell, MA 01851
www.classiceliteyarns.com
- Meandering Vine Shawl, pg 40
- Men's Vest, pg. 90
- Fair Isle Style Pillow, pg. 116

Dale of Norway
N16 W23390 Stoneridge Dr #A
Waukesha, WI 53188
www.daleofnorway.com
- Posy Tote, pg. 48
- Celtic Moss Sweater, pg. 74

Harrisville Designs
PO Box 806
Harrisville, NH 03450
www.harrisville.com
- Easy Falling Snow Hat, pg. 26

Koigu
RR# 1 Williamsford, Ontario,
Canada N0H 2V0
www.koigu.com
- Petite Smocked Bag, pg. 56

Lorna's Laces Yarns
4229 N Honore St
Chicago, IL 60613
www.lornaslaces.net
- Norwegian Ski Sweater, pg. 70

Louisa Harding
www.knittingfever.com
- Sparkling Leaves Hat, pg. 24
- Ribbon Scarf, pg. 30

Mountain Colors Yarn
PO Box 156
Corvallis, MT 59828
www.mountaincolors.com
- Red Sweater, pg. 102

Plymouth Yarn
P.O. Box 28
Bristol, PA 19007
www.plymouthyarn.com
- Ocean Waves Cotton Tank,
 pg. 86

Rowan, Jaeger
Westminster Fibers
4 Townsend W Unit 8
Nashua, NH 03063
- Crazy Quilt Stripes Bag, pg. 52
- Blanket, pg. 120

Tahki/StacyCharles
S. Charles Collezione
70-30 80th St., Building 36
Ridgewood, NY 11384
www.tahkistacycharles.com
- Little Black Purse, pg. 46
- Tunic Sweater Jacket, pg. 94
- Easy Polka-Dot Pillow, pg. 108

Trendsetter Yarns
16745 Saticoy St, #101
Van Nuys, CA 91406
www.trendsetteryarns.com
- Ocean Ermine Scarf, pg. 32

Beads and Embroidery Supplies

I encourage you to find your beads at local bead stores and your embroidery supplies at local embroidery stores as much as possible. Nothing beats being able to see the colors and match them to your yarn. And it's important to keep local stores in business if you want to have them available.

If you can't find what you are looking for, here is the store where I buy most of my beads:

Here is a great store for embroidery supplies:

Creative Castle
2321 Michael Drive
Newbury Park, CA 92320
(805) 499-1377
www.creativecastle.com

Weavers Needle and Frame
1610 Newbury Road, Suite 2
Thousand Oaks, CA 91320
 Phone 805-499-7979
 Fax 805-499-5184
 www.weavers.needle@verizon.net

This wonderful yarn store has many of the projects from this book, and others I have written, on display:

Anacapa Fine Yarns
4572 Telephone Road #909
Ventura, CA 93003
(805) 654-9500
www.anacapafineyarns.com

Index